CULTURES OF THE WORLD
Germany

Cavendish
Square

New York

Published in 2014 by Cavendish Square Publishing, LLC
303 Park Avenue South, Suite 1247, New York, NY 10010

Third Edition

This publication is published with arrangement with Marshall Cavendish International (Asia) Pte Ltd.

Website: cavendishsq.com

Cultures of the World is a registered trademark of Times Publishing Limited.

This publication represents the opinions and views of the author based on his or her personal experience, knowledge, and research. The information in this book serves as a general guide only. The author and publisher have used their best efforts in preparing this book and disclaim liability rising directly or indirectly from the use and application of this book.

CPSIA Compliance Information: Batch #WS13CSQ

All websites were available and accurate when this book was sent to press.

Library of Congress Cataloging-in-Publication Data
Fuller, Barbara, 1961–
   Germany / Barbara Fuller, Gabriele Vossmeyer, Yong Jui Lin. — 3rd ed.
      p. cm. — (Cultures of the world)
   Includes bibliographical references and index.
   Summary: Provides comprehensive information on the geography, history,
wildlife, governmental structure, economy, cultural diversity, peoples,
religion, and culture of Germany"—Provided by publisher.
   ISBN 978-1-60870-868-0 (hardcover) ISBN 978-1-62712-159-0 (paperback) ISBN 978-1-60870-874-1 (ebook)
   1. Germany—Juvenile literature. I. Vossmeyer, Gabriele. II. Yong, Jui Lin.
III. Title.

   DD17.F85 2013
   943—dc23   2012017632

Writers: Barbara Fuller, Gabriele Vossmeyer, Yong Jui Lin
Editors: Deborah Grahame-Smith, Mindy Pang
Copyreader: Tara Tomczyk
Designers: Nancy Sabato, Benson Tan
Cover picture researcher: Tracey Engel
Picture researcher: Joshua Ang

PRECEDING PAGE
Forggensee Lake located in Füssen, Ostallgäu.

Printed in the United States of America

CONTENTS

GERMANY TODAY **5**

1. GEOGRAPHY North German Lowlands • Central Highlands • Alps and pre-Alps • The Rhine • East and West • States • Cities • Climate • Flora and fauna **11**

2. HISTORY Early history • The Middle Ages • The Hapsburg dynasty • 19th-century Germany • World War I • The Weimar Republic • The Hitler years • Postwar Germany • East—West German relations • Reunification **27**

3. GOVERNMENT Federal government • State governments • Political parties • The legal system **41**

4. ECONOMY Postwar economic miracle • Infrastructure and communications • Industries • Agriculture • Germany and Europe • Banking and finance • East and West disparities • Working life **47**

5. ENVIRONMENT Environmental legislation • Renewable Energy Resources Law • Air pollution • Noise and water pollution • Flood prevention • Recycling • An end to nuclear power • The way forward • National parks and reserves in Germany **57**

6. GERMANS German characteristics • Dress • Immigrants and minorities • Class divisions **65**

7. LIFESTYLE Housing • Family life • Childhood rituals • Youth • Weddings • Deaths • Women • Shopping • Education • Health care **71**

8. RELIGION Church in society • Catholicism • Protestantism • Other beliefs **81**

9. LANGUAGE The German language • Script • Pronunciation • High and Low German • Forms of address • Body language and etiquette **87**

10. ARTS Music • Great musicians • Jazz • Pop and rock • Movies • Theater • Literature • Philosophy • Fine arts • Architecture **95**

11. LEISURE Sports • Soccer • The great outdoors • Winter sports • At home • Vacations **109**

12. FESTIVALS Carnival • The Munich Oktoberfest • Other drinking festivals • Christian festivals • Processions • Other festivals **117**

13. FOOD Local specialties • Meals • Eating out • Alcohol **125**

MAP OF GERMANY **132**

ABOUT THE ECONOMY **135**

ABOUT THE CULTURE **137**

TIMELINE **138**

GLOSSARY **140**

FOR FURTHER INFORMATION **141**

BIBLIOGRAPHY **142**

INDEX **143**

GERMANY TODAY

WITH 81.2 MILLION INHABITANTS (2013 ESTIMATE), GERMANY is the most populous member state and the largest economy in the European Union (EU). It is the third-largest importer of goods in the world. The country has developed a very high standard of living and a comprehensive system of social security. Germany has been the home of many influential scientists and inventors, and it is known for its rich cultural and political history.

It is one of the major political powers of Europe and a technological leader in many fields. Free of the economic malaise that seems to be gripping most of the other EU countries, Germany is seen as the white knight galloping to the rescue of debt-crippled countries such as Greece. However, given its Nazi past as well as the austerity measures that come with the financial aid, Germany sometimes does not get the welcome one would expect but instead is greeted with resentment and insults.

After losing two disastrous World Wars in the last century, Germany has risen like a phoenix from the ashes. After World War II, Germany was divided into East and West Germany. German reunification came about on October 3, 1990 with the fall of the Berlin Wall. Most of the kinks in the uneasy marriage of East and West Germany appeared to have been ironed out. As part of the Berlin/Bonn Act, adopted on April 26, 1994, Berlin became the capital of the reunified Germany.

Germany's climate is temperate and marine, with cool, cloudy, and wet winters and summers. The greater part of Germany lies in the cool climatic zone in which humid westerly winds predominate. In the northwest and the north, the climate is extremely oceanic, and rain falls year-round. Winters there are relatively mild and summers comparatively cool. In the east, the climate shows clear continental features. Winters can be very cold for long periods, and summers can become very warm. Dry periods are often recorded.

Germany is known for its many zoological gardens, wildlife parks, aquariums, and bird parks. More than 400 registered zoos and animal parks operate in Germany, which is believed to be the largest number in any single country of the world. The Zoologischer Garten Berlin is the oldest zoo in Germany and presents the most comprehensive collection of species in the world.

The United Nations Population Fund lists Germany as host to the third-highest number of international migrants worldwide. Around 20 percent of Germany's population do not hold a German passport or are descendents of immigrants. Germany has a number of large cities. The most populous are Berlin, Hamburg, Munich, Cologne, Frankfurt, and Stuttgart. The largest conurbation is the Rhine—Ruhr region (11 million residents), which includes Düsseldorf (the capital of North Rhine—Westphalia), Cologne, Essen, Dortmund, Duisburg, and Bochum.

With one in three young children born in Germany coming from an immigrant background, Germany is quickly becoming even more diverse. Germany has an integration commissioner, which indicates how serious the country is about integrating immigrants into society. However, deep barriers remain. Migrants are now more likely to attend university-preparatory high schools than in previous years, but as a whole they are still not on par with their German counterparts in this regard. Of immigrant youth, 43 percent get only as far as Germany's basic school-leaving certificate, compared with 31 percent of ethnic Germans. Thirteen percent of non-Germans aged 15 to 18 drop out of school altogether. On average, it takes 17 months for a young person with an immigrant background to secure an apprenticeship or traineeship, whereas ethnic Germans, on average, need just three months. So far, the federal government has promised an extra €15 million for integration courses. The integration commissioner is also pushing a bill for better recognition of foreign degrees and professional accreditation and is seeking legislation to make education more accessible.

Germans have not forgotten that their country was the author of the horrors of the 1930s and 1940s, but Renate Kocher of Allensbach, a polling firm, says they want to "draw a line under the past." That

The thrice rebuilt Hohenzollern Castle on top of Mount Hohenzollern stands 2,805 feet (855 m) above sea level.

does not mean ignoring its lessons or neglecting to teach them to the next generation. The exhibition "Hitler and the Germans" at the German Historical Museum in Berlin drew blockbuster crowds. But Germans are no longer so ready to be put on the moral defensive or to view the Nazi era as the defining episode of their past. Even non-Germans seem willing to move on, as recent books such as *The German Genius: Europe's Third Renaissance, the Second Scientific Revolution, and the 20th Century* suggest. Germany still atones for its past crimes, but now it also preaches on the evils of debt, the importance of nurturing industry, and the superiority of long-term thinking in enterprise. By the end of 2011, Germany was estimated to have made more than €9 billion out of the eurozone crisis as investors flocked to safer German federal government bonds.

According to a survey conducted by the University of Leipzig in 2010, a high number of Germans agree with xenophobic statements. For instance, 32 percent of Germans approve of the statement: "When there's a shortage of jobs, foreigners should be sent back home." Thirty four percent agree with the statement: "Foreigners only come here to exploit Germany's social welfare system." And 35 percent think: "Germany has a dangerous level of foreign influence as a result of the many foreigners in the country." A third of those surveyed think the country is overrun by foreigners, and a majority favor "sharply restricting" Muslim religious practice. More than 10 percent would even welcome a führer who would govern with "a strong hand"—a sign that the embers of extremism still glow. One can slowly see the undercurrents of anti-Semitism in German society being replaced by Islamophobia.

Conservative politicians in Germany are pandering to this Islamophobia. Horst Seehofer, head of the Christian Social Union, the Bavarian sister party of the ruling Christian Democratic Union (CDU), declared in October 2010 that Germany needs no further immigration from Turkey or the Arab world, citing the difficulties Muslim immigrants have integrating into German society. Characteristically, Angela Merkel, the German chancellor, sought to placate anti-immigrant sentiment without stooping to popular sentiment. Multiculturalism has "absolutely failed," she said on October 16 of the same year, implying that immigrants would be expected to integrate better into German society. But she balanced this by admitting that Islam "is part of Germany."

It might seem that life in Germany is harsh, with half of one's income going to taxes and stores being closed on Sundays. But most Germans enjoy a high standard of living compared with people in other countries. They are entitled to four weeks of vacation (24 vacation days for those working a six-day week; 20 vacation days for those with the standard five-day workweek), plus 9—13 official holidays per year. Germany ranks third after the United States and Switzerland for the highest per capita income in the world, and it has a literacy rate of 99 percent. Home ownership, however, is low at 42 percent with many Germans preferring to rent. As of late 2012, unemployment was at 6.5 percent (compared with 24 percent in Greece).

Germany has 36 UNESCO World Heritage Sites. The three natural sites are the German Beech Forests, the Wadden Sea, and the Messel Pit Fossil Site. The beech forests are in the states of Mecklenburg-Vorpommern (Jasmund and Müritz National Parks), Brandenburg (Grumsiner Forest), Thuringia (Hainich National Park), and Hesse (Kellerwald-Edersee National Park). Some of the trees are 400 years old, and some parts of these forests remain largely untouched by humans. The forest in Hainich National Park was a military exclusion zone for 40 years, and hardly anyone was allowed to enter it.

The Wadden Sea consists of the Dutch Wadden Sea Conservation Area and the German Wadden Sea National Parks of Lower Saxony and Schleswig-

Holstein. It is a large temperate, relatively flat coastal wetland environment, formed by the intricate interactions among physical and biological factors that have given rise to a multitude of transitional habitats with tidal channels, sandy shoals, sea-grass meadows, mussel beds, sandbars, mudflats, salt marshes, estuaries, beaches, and dunes. The site is home to numerous plant and animal species, including marine mammals such as the harbor seal, the gray seal, and the harbor porpoise. It is also a breeding and wintering area for up to 12 million birds each year. The site is one of the last remaining natural, large-scale, intertidal ecosystems where natural processes continue to function largely undisturbed.

Men and women dressed in traditional outfits in Munich.

Messel Pit is the richest site in the world for understanding the living environment of the Eocene period, between 56 million and 34 million years ago. In particular, it provides unique information about the early stages of the evolution of mammals and includes exceptionally well preserved mammal fossils, ranging from fully articulated skeletons to the contents of animals' stomachs.

Germany is a land full of culinary delights. The Christian calendar is a map for German social events, and there is always a celebration happening somewhere, with food specialties, presents, and homemade entertainment. Cozy gatherings with food and drink are the essence of German comfort and hospitality.

Today Germans still fall back on their rich heritage, serving wild game, lamb, pork, and beef with old and new ways of preparing them and their side dishes. Popular spices are mustard, horseradish, and juniper berries. Modern German chefs have started to create newer, lighter fare, incorporating traditional foods into their menus, such as serving sauerkraut with cod or reducing salad dressing in potato salads.

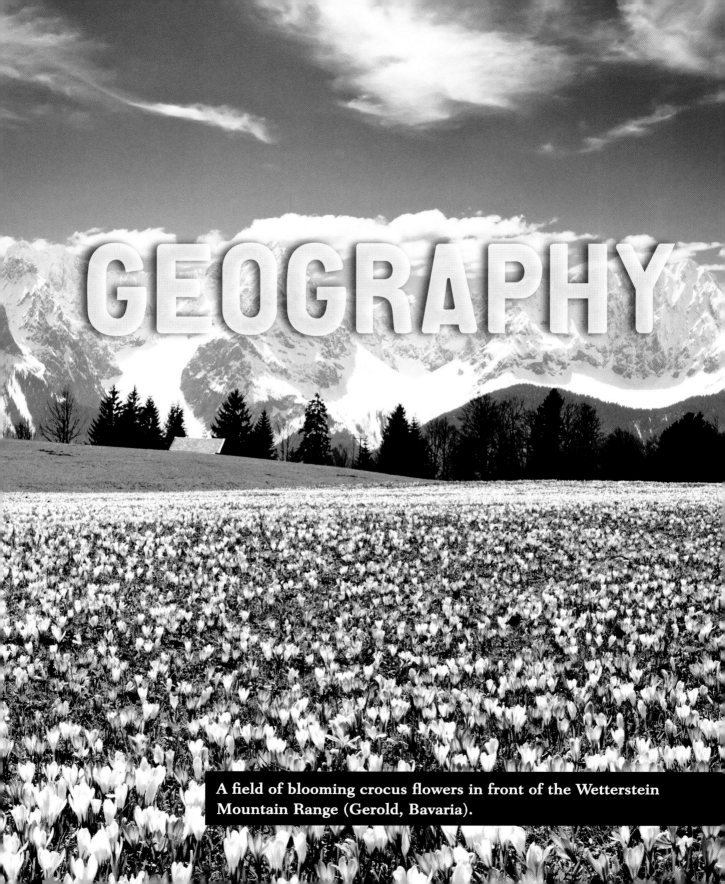

GEOGRAPHY

A field of blooming crocus flowers in front of the Wetterstein Mountain Range (Gerold, Bavaria).

THE ALPS ARE GERMANY'S MOST prominent geographical feature. Unlike other mountain ranges in the world, the Alps do not form an unbroken chain. Instead the range is divided by many deep valleys.

Scientists believe that during the last ice age (about 18,000 years ago), glaciers from Scandinavia and northern Europe advanced onto central Europe and covered the entire continent, including the Alps. As glaciers melted, distinctive marks were left across Europe's terrain.

The beautiful Eschenlohe of Garmisch-Partenkirchen in Bavaria boasts a view of the Loisachtal Valley, the Ester Range, the Wetterstein Range, and the Ammergau Alps.

1

Germany has the second largest population in Europe (after the European part of Russia) and is the seventh largest in area in Europe.

The force of the glaciers' retreat widened the gaps between the mountains in the Alps. This created numerous U-shape valleys. Deep, enclosed valleys were filled with water, created elongated lakes such as Constance. Melting water from the mountaintops poured forth to the valleys below produced enormous waterfalls. The retreating glaciers also carried huge amounts of gravel and debris, which were eventually deposited into the valleys as the glaciers melted away.

The physical features acquired by the Alps during the last ice age have given the Alpine terrain its characteristic unevenness. Thus the Alps divide Germany into three distinct regions: the North German Lowlands, the Central Highlands, and the Alps and the Alpine Foreland.

The geological characteristics of each region actually cover an area farther east and west than Germany's current borders. The lowlands, for example, stretch west into the Netherlands and Belgium and east through Poland's Silesian Plains to as far as the Ural Mountains in Russia. The Oder River and the Neisse River provide a natural border with Poland, the Alps provide a natural border with Switzerland and Austria, and the Rhine River in the south and southwest forms a natural border with France.

Crossing the Oder River, the Oder Bridge links Frankfurt to Słubice in Poland.

The Farver Mühle historic mill in Schleswig-Holstein.

NORTH GERMAN LOWLANDS

The North Sea coast is Germany's most important shipping outlet. The land along the coast is extremely flat and shallow, and close to sea level. Dikes have therefore been built to protect the land from floods.

Several islands are located off the north coast including the East Frisian Islands and Helgoland. The latter was formerly used as a naval base but has become a haven for the study of birds. Hamburg, located on the Elbe River, and Bremerhaven, located on the Weser River, are major ports. Smaller ports such as Wilhelmshaven and Emden on the northwestern tip are also important.

The Baltic coast is a mixture of flat sandy shores and steep cliffs, with shallow natural inlets for ports. In the northernmost part of the country, the Nord-Ostsee Canal links the Baltic to the North Sea. South of the Baltic Sea, a fertile belt runs from Holstein to Mecklenburg. Brandenburg's low-lying plains alternate with wide marshy valleys.

CENTRAL HIGHLANDS

The Central Highlands is a complex region that consists of a great variety of geographical features: high plains, undulating hills, mountain ranges, and wide river courses.

Germany's largest slate mountains, the Rhineland Schiefergebirge, run across the northwestern part of the country and are bisected by the Rhine River. These mountains in turn are made up of the Eifel Range of 50 cone-shape extinct volcanoes, the exposed stony plateau of the Hunsrück region, the agricultural areas of Sauerland and Bergisches Land, the Rothaargebirge Range, the forested area known as Westerwald, and the heavily wooded Taunus region.

The Ruhr industrial area, where iron ore and hard coal deposits have led to the development of huge steel industries, lies partly to the east of the Rhine and north of the Schiefergebirge.

East of the Rhineland lies the Hesse Central Upland, which includes the Vogelsberg Range. To the northeast of these mountains is the Harz Range, the site of numerous reservoirs. The east and south slopes of the Harz descend into the Thuringian Basin, an extremely fertile region. Here grains such as wheat and barley as well as root crops are grown in the flat areas. Orchards and vineyards are found on slopes overlooking the Ilm River.

The Erzgebirge Range, found south of the Thuringian Basin, forms a natural border with the Czech Republic. The range is also known as the Ore Mountains, named for the silver and tin mines found here in the 16th century that were exploited until recent years. The city of Dresden sits on the plain beneath these mountains.

THE SOUTHERN HIGHLANDS South of the Schiefergebirge lies the wide Rhine floodplain. The plain enjoys a mild climate, making it extremely fertile. Fruit orchards are planted on the western hills from Frankfurt to Heidelberg. The nearby Neckar Valley, on the other hand, has areas devoted to industry as well as agriculture. Two of the world's most famous forests lie to the south of the Central Uplands: the Black Forest in the southwest and the Bavarian Forest in the southeast. The Black Forest, named for its numerous dark fir trees, is the source of the Danube and Neckar rivers. The Bavarian Forest is covered mainly with coniferous trees. The national park located here is the largest of its kind in Central Europe.

ALPS AND PRE-ALPS

The Danube, rising in the Black Forest and leaving Germany at Passau in the east on its way to the Black Sea, runs along the northern edge of the Alpine foreland, which rises to an average height of 5,412 feet (1,640 meters). Popular lakes such as the Chiemsee, the Starnberger See, and the Ammersee are found in this area.

The Sankt Märgen Black Forest in Baden-Württemberg.

A view of Frauenchiemsee Island on the Chiemsee freshwater lake in Bavaria.

In the northern part of the region, Lower Bavaria's fertile soil is ideal for the production of hops, which are grown for the breweries in nearby Munich. Small marshes, where the water table is high, are also found here. The southern part of the region is higher and wetter, thereby suitable for raising cattle. Augsburg and Munich are the main population centers of the region.

In the southwest, Lake Constance, measuring 39 miles (63 kilometers) long and 8.7 miles (14 km) wide, is nestled in the depression of Alpine fallout moraines (irregular masses of boulders and gravel). Along with the Chiemsee, Lake Constance makes up part of the Alpine lakes. This is the focus of considerable settlement, a booming tourism industry, and is home to institutions devoted to scientific studies.

The German Alps are found to the east of Lake Constance and at the border with Austria. From west to east, they are divided into the Allgäu, the Bavarian, and the Berchtesgaden Alps. The north-facing Alpine slopes are forested, and farms with pastureland dot the south-facing slopes. The lower slopes have mixed forests, its conifers lie between 3,000 and 5,600 feet (914 and 1,707 m). Year-round, snow is present above 8,500 feet (2,591 m). The Zugspitze, at 9,725 feet (2,964 m), is Germany's highest mountain. Nearby Garmisch-Partenkirchen is the country's major ski resort.

THE RHINE

The Rhine River is 766 miles (1,233 km) long, the second longest in Europe. It originates in the Swiss Alps and flows northward to the North Sea. The river forms a natural border between Germany and Switzerland from Lake Constance to the Swiss town of Basel, continuing between France and Germany from Basel to Karlsruhe. Breathtaking vineyards, fortresses, castles, and picturesque towns line the banks of the Rhine.

The river is navigable for about 540 miles (870 km). It is the busiest waterway in Europe—ships traveling on the Rhine carry 183.6 million tons (166.6 million metric tons) of cargo every year. In the Alps the river moves rapidly, turning into spectacular waterfalls at Schaffhausen, Switzerland. It then opens onto a wide plateau from Karlsruhe to Mainz, where crops are grown along its banks. North of Mainz, the river plunges into a gorge through the Schiefergebirge before opening out into a wider floodplain to the north of Koblenz, the traditional wine-growing region. Between Cologne and the Dutch border, the Rhine flows through the Ruhr industrial area.

An aerial view of the bridges joining the Moselle and Rhine rivers in Rhineland-Palatinate.

EAST AND WEST

The division of the country into East Germany, or, the Deutsche Demokratische Republik, and West Germany, or, the Bundesrepublik Deutschland (BRD), between 1945 and 1990 affected every part of German life and geography. Even today Germany is still in a phase of rapid change.

Agricultural development, landholding patterns, industrial practice, housing, and forms of law enforcement and government all differed greatly from East to West.

Environmental concerns about industrial pollution and long overdue efforts to preserve historical buildings, maintain housing in adequate condition, and restore properties seized by the former East German state from their owners are just some of the issues Germany has been trying to resolve. Social and economic problems are arising from different attitudes toward work, wealth, goals, and standard of living between the two regions.

The Hessischer Landtag in Wiesbaden is the political center of the state of Hesse in Germany.

East Germany was the part of Germany that came under Soviet rule at the end of World War II. This area had suffered some of the worst wartime bomb damage and was also forced to make extremely demanding compensation payments to the Allied nations for Germany's actions in the war. It experienced an almost immediate population drain to West Germany after World War II.

During the early 1950s, the border between the two states was guarded by watchtowers and barbed wire from the eastern side. Yet a steady stream of emigrants, totaling about 3.5 million, continued to leave through Berlin. On August 13, 1961, an 11-foot-high (3.3-m-high) concrete wall was constructed overnight, dividing the communist East from the West. The wall became a symbol of the oppression of the East German regime, turning the former capital into a divided city, as the main street, Unter den Linden, was blocked by part of the 40-mile (64-km) barrier. At least 72 people died attempting to cross the wall, 55 of whom were shot by East German security forces. The last victim, Chris Gueffroy, was shot in February 1989.

In the late 1980s popular protests began, ending with the fall of the Communist government and the opening of the wall on November 9, 1989. When the wall opened, a flood of Germans from both East and West streamed through. Germany reunification was formally concluded on October 3, 1990. Parts of the wall still stand in some places in Berlin, and a section of it is on display at the Berlin Wall Memorial and Documentation Center.

STATES

Germany is made up of 16 states that are referred to as *Länder* (Lenn-DOR). Each state has its own constitution and is largely autonomous in regard to its internal organization. The states and their capitals are as follows: Baden-Württemberg, with Stuttgart; Bavaria, with Munich; Berlin, with Berlin; Brandenburg, with Potsdam; Bremen, with Bremen; Hamburg, with Hamburg; Hesse, with Wiesbaden; Mecklenburg-Vorpommern, with Schwerin; Lower Saxony, with Hannover; North Rhine-Westphalia, with Düsseldorf; Rhineland-Palatinate, with Mainz; Saarland, with Saarbrücken; Saxony, with Dresden; Saxony-Anhalt, with Magdeburg; Schleswig-Holstein, with Kiel; Thuringia, with Erfurt.

CITIES

There is no single dominant city in Germany, as most have a strong tradition of local self-government. Wealth, industry, and cultural activities are spread throughout the entire country, preventing the common problem of overconcentration of resources in one area at the expense of others.

BERLIN Berlin is the capital of Germany and is also one of its 16 states. With a population of 3.5 million people, Berlin is Germany's largest city.

Berlin's economy is primarily based on the service sector, encompassing a diverse range of creative industries, media corporations, and convention venues. Berlin also serves as a continental hub for air and rail transport and is a popular tourist destination. Significant industries include information technology, pharmaceuticals, biomedical engineering, biotechnology, electronics, traffic engineering, and renewable energy.

Berlin is home to renowned universities, research institutes, orchestras, museums, and celebrities, as well as host of many sporting events. Its urban settings and historical legacy have made it a popular location for international film productions.

A cultural and intellectual city, Munich is famous for its breweries and *Weissbier* (also known as *Weizenbier*), or wheat beer, which is a specialty from Bavaria.

MUNICH Munich is the third largest city in Germany, after Berlin and Hamburg. About 1.35 million people live within the city limits. The city center is only one mile (1.6 km) across, and no skyscrapers are allowed to interrupt the original styles of architecture. Munich hosted the 1972 Olympics. Its sports and leisure facilities are excellent, as is its transportation system. Siemens, one of the world's leading electrical engineering and electronics companies, BMW, and MBB Aerospace are based in Munich.

STUTTGART Set in a picturesque hollow of terraced suburbs surrounded by vineyards and forested hills, Stuttgart feels small despite a surrounding industrial area that houses major companies such as Bosch, Daimler AG, Porsche, and German IBM. The downtown area is relatively new, as it was rebuilt after World War II. Stuttgart has a famous ballet troupe, several foreign consulates, and inviting open-air cafés along the Schlossplatz, the central pedestrian zone. The sixth largest city in Germany, Stuttgart has a population of 606,588 people, while the metropolitan area has a population of 5.3 million.

Stuttgart is spread across a variety of hills (some of them vineyards), valleys, and parks— unusual for a German city and often a source of surprise to visitors, who primarily associate the city with its industrial reputation as the "cradle of the automobile."

Autumn light shines on a vineyard in Stuttgart.

An evening view of the skyline in Frankfurt, dominated by towering and brightly lit skyscapers.

FRANKFURT AM MAIN Frankfurt am Main, commonly known as Frankfurt, is the fifth largest city in Germany. In 2012, the city boasted a population of 704,449. It is the financial and transportation center of Germany and the largest financial hub in continental Europe. The city has been a banking center since the 16th century. The German Stock Exchange, the headquarters of most German banks, and the European Central Bank are located in Frankfurt's city center. The city's trade revenue supports a generous budget for the arts, architecture, and conservation. It is also a publishing center and the host of the largest annual international book fair every October. Frankfurt is an international city with a bright intellectual life. Twenty-two percent of its population are immigrant workers. The city also operates the largest airport in Germany and one of the busiest in Europe. Frankfurt lies in the former American Occupation Zone of Germany and was formerly the headquarters of the U.S. Army in Germany.

BONN was the capital of West Germany from 1949 to 1990 and the official seat of government of united Germany from 1990 to 1999. Bonn currently hosts 17 United Nations institutions and is the seat of some of Germany's largest corporate players chiefly in the areas of telecommunications and logistics. The city is establishing itself as an important national and international center of meetings, conventions, and conferences, many of which are directly related to the work of the United Nations.

COLOGNE is Germany's fourth largest city (after Berlin, Hamburg, and Munich). During World War II, Cologne was a Military Area Command Headquarters for the Nazis and endured 262 air raids by the Western Allies which resulted in approximately 20,000 civilian casualties and almost wiped out the center of the city. By the end of the war, the population of Cologne had been reduced by 95 percent. By 1959 the city's population reached prewar numbers again, and the population exceeded 1 million by mid-2010. Cologne is a major cultural center of the Rhineland and has a vibrant arts scene.

HAMBURG is the second largest city in Germany. Situated on the Elbe River, it is the third largest port in Europe (after Rotterdam and Antwerp). Hamburg is built on water and has 2,195 bridges that cross over the Elbe, Lake Alster, and many canals. The lake freezes over during the winter. There are few high-rise buildings in the city center, which makes use of mostly red-brick architecture, and the tallest buildings are approximately 30 stories.

DRESDEN Dresden has a long history as the capital and royal residence for the electors and kings of Saxony, who for centuries furnished the city with cultural and artistic splendor. The city was known as the Jewel Box because of its baroque and rococo city center. A controversial Allied aerial bombing toward the end of World War II killed thousands of civilians and destroyed the city center. The impact of the bombing and 40 years of urban development during the East German Communist era have considerably changed the face of the city. Some restoration work has helped to reconstruct parts of the historic inner city including the Katholische Hofkirche, the Semperoper, and the Dresdner Frauenkirche. Since the German reunification in 1990, Dresden has regained importance as one of the cultural, educational, political, and economic centers of Germany.

Fellhorn Mountain in the Allgäu Alps near Oberstdorf is well known for its fields of Alp roses.

CLIMATE

The northwest region of Germany has an Atlantic climate similar to that of the American Northwest: westerly winds, cool summers, moderate winters, high humidity, and high annual rainfall.

In the northeast, the winters are bitterly cold as the area receives the force of the Russian winds. Summers are hot with relatively low rainfall.

The Alpine region is characterized by warm but short summers and cold, snowy winters. Mild, warm winds, known as foehns, blowing in from the south are responsible for the melting of snow at the end of winter.

The climate in the Rhine Rift Valley, which has early springs, light rainfall, warm summers, and few frosts, is ideal for agriculture as well as tourism. Average January temperatures are 37°F (3°C) in the lowlands and 21°F (-6°C) in the mountains. In the summer, the temperatures are between 68°F (20°C) and 86°F (30°C). The average annual rainfall is 23.7 inches (603 millimeters). September is the driest month in Germany.

FLORA AND FAUNA

Forests cover 32 percent of Germany, and all are open to the public. Forests that receive enough light and have good soil offer favorable conditions for the growth of dog's mercury, sweet woodruff, and violets. At higher levels, balsam, willow herb, monkshood, bilberry, foxglove, and wavy hair grass are found.

In 1980 the first signs of pollution became evident when trees were found to be dying. Acid rain caused by sulfur dioxide emissions from industry was believed to be the reason. These dying forests are one of Germany's most important ecological issues. Regulations to reduce pollution caused by cars have been introduced to try to prevent further damage, and renewable energy now accounts for more than 14 percent of Germany's electricity consumption.

The government has strict antipollution laws. Industries face heavy fines for discharging poisonous emissions. The Rhine River and its valley underwent a successful cleanup campaign: the waters of the river were made clean enough for the pollution-sensitive salmon to grow and thrive. In addition, various nature conservation groups advised using natural rather than chemical pesticides to rid the area of insects.

Some of the former border territories between East and West Germany have been turned into nature reserves. A 5,683-acre (2,300-hectare) area along Lake Schaal between Schleswig-Holstein and Mecklenburg hosts sea eagles, cranes, cormorants, bitterns, graylag geese, ospreys, and other birds. Much of the Lüneburg Heath region in the northeast, an area of 436 square miles (1,130 square km), is a nature reserve, as is the Bavarian National Park. A little known fact is that Germany has a high population of deer and boar that are managed for hunting. Wild deer are also found in mountainous areas, such as the Harz Mountains and the Alpine foothills. The German Alps are full of romantic castles and picturesque lakes.

The marshland near the mouth of the Elbe is fertile, but further inland it becomes sandy, with boulders, heath, peat bogs, fens, and marshes. This infertile plain includes two major cities, Hannover and Brunswick.

INTERNET LINKS

www.mygermancity.com/german-alps

Provides a beautiful review of the German Alps and its castles, lakes, and other points of interest.

www.newseum.org/berlinwall/

Newseum is an interactive website where one can find out more about the Berlin Wall.

www.germany.travel/en/index.html

Germany's official tourism website provides comprehensive information about traveling in the country.

HISTORY

The 19th-century Schloss Neuschwanstein palace stands on a rugged hill above the village of Hohenschwangau in Bavaria.

2

THE HISTORY OF GERMANY as a nation is relatively short, since the country was first united as recently as 1871. The history of the German people, however, dates back to ancient times.

EARLY HISTORY

During the Bronze Age, Germanic peoples probably inhabited southern Scandinavia and northern Germany. Around the first century A.D., the Roman Empire attempted to expand its territory in the northeast, but

The Saalburg, a reconstruction of a Limes Germanicus Roman fort.

The region that is known as Germany today became associated with the name *Germany* in the first century B.C., when the conquest of Gaul made the Romans aware that there was an ethnic and linguistic distinction between the Celts (or Gauls) and their aggressive neighbors, the German tribes.

the invaders were driven away by the German Cherusci tribe leader Arminius in A.D. 9. The Romans tried to keep the Germanic tribes at bay by using the Rhine and Danube rivers as natural barriers, further reinforcing these with a 342-mile-long (550-km-long) wall called the Limes. Parts of this wall can still be seen today.

The arrival of the Huns at the end of the first century forced the migration of Germanic tribes—Ostrogoths, Visigoths, and Vandals—into Roman territory, in what became known as the *Völkerwanderung* (FOLL-ker-van-der-ung). The Vandals crossed the Rhine River in A.D. 46, later bringing an end to Roman rule in the region. The Vandals, Goths, and other Germanic tribes settled there in the second half of the fourth century.

At the end of the fifth century, the neighboring Franks under the Merovingian king, Clovis I, expanded political control over territories from northern Spain and the Atlantic coast to the Rhine, converting all the people to Christianity. By the beginning of the eighth century, the Franks had conquered all the Germanic tribes except the Saxons.

An artist's impression of soldiers herding the defeated Germanic tribes before a Roman commander.

A wood carving of Otto I the Great in his court.

THE MIDDLE AGES

Charlemagne, known in Germany as Karl der Grosse (ruled 768—814), was crowned Holy Roman Emperor by the pope in A.D. 800. He conquered the Saxons and converted them to Christianity in 805. After Charlemagne's death, the kingdom of the Eastern Franks became the Germanic kingdom under his grandson Ludwig the German (ruled 843—76). The area of the Western Franks became what is now France. The land in the middle, Lotharingia, became Lorraine.

Later, another German king, Otto I the Great (912—73), defeated the Hungarian Magyars at Lechfeld in 955, conquered northern Italy, and was crowned Holy Roman Emperor of German nations in 962. From then until 1806, all German kings were given this title. The church became an administrative part of the empire, gaining wealth, land, and importance. In 1806, following a defeat by Napoleon, the French emperor, the Holy Roman Empire of German Nations was dissolved.

Under Heinrich IV (ruled 1056—1106), a dispute arose with the pope, leading to a split of the Christian empire and disunity among the German princes within the Germanic kingdom. Friedrich I of the Hohenstaufen dynasty, also known as Barbarossa (ruled 1155—90), started wars against the pope, the Italians, and the Saxons, but the rise of individual German princes

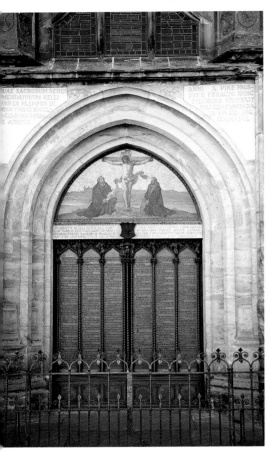

and dukes weakened the dynasty and led to the end of the Hohenstaufen era in 1268. The kings eventually became a pawn of the powerful aristocrats. Throughout the 12th and 13th centuries, Germanic influence increased east of the Elbe River, and Teutonic knights spread Christianity along most of the Baltic coasts. In 1356 the empire established rules for electing the king of Germany. Princes and dukes had votes, as did several archbishops and some important towns.

THE HAPSBURG DYNASTY

With the rise of the Hapsburg dynasty in Austria, political power in Germany shifted to eastern Germany, but the Rhineland princes and dukes continued to exert political influence. The Hapsburg dynasty also increased the emperor's powers. Rudolf I (ruled 1273—91) virtually controlled Germany and Austria. The next Hapsburg rulers, Maximilian I (ruled 1493—1519) and his grandson Charles V (ruled 1519—56), were both powerful Holy Roman emperors.

In 1517, during the Hapsburg reign, Martin Luther, a friar, wrote *The Ninety-Five Theses* to protest the various

The church door at Wittenberg, where Martin Luther allegedly posted his *Ninety-Five Theses*.

abuses in the Catholic Church, in particular the sale of "indulgences" for the forgiveness of sins. Luther's strong criticism of the Church sparked the Protestant Reformation.

Many princes and dukes became Protestant, and religious wars were fought until the Peace of Augsburg, which allowed Protestants the same rights of worship as Catholics, was signed in 1555. Although four-fifths of Germany had become Protestant, the ratio changed after many of the abuses were corrected during the Counter Reformation started by the Council of Trent (1545—63).

Peace did not last long. The Thirty Years' War (1618—48), fueled by religious hatred within Europe—in particular, Sweden, Austria, and France—ended with the Treaty of Westphalia. But the war reduced the population by one-third. The treaty removed much of the remaining power of the Hapsburg kings.

It also deprived Germany of access to the sea, leaving 1,800 independent kingdoms. Some of the rulers of these kingdoms, including Frederick the Great of Prussia (ruled 1740—86) and Joseph II of Austria (ruled 1764—90), encouraged humanistic inquiry.

An engraving of the Swedes invading Munich in 1632 during the Thirty Years' War.

19TH-CENTURY GERMANY

The French Revolution of 1789 had its effect on Germany. When Berlin and the left bank of the Rhine River were occupied during the Napoleonic Wars and the last Holy Roman emperor, Franz II, was forced from the throne in 1806, the fires of German nationalism were lit. Germany's so-called particularism—that is, the existence within it of many states of various sizes—persisted until 1871, when the country was finally united. This has become the basis of the current German *Länder* (state) structure.

The Congress of Vienna convened in 1815 at the end of the Napoleonic Wars. For nine months, the congress strove to redraw the political boundaries of Europe. The German Confederation, a union of 39 states that included Austria, was formed out of up to 350 separate German states and territories. In 1834 the German Customs Union was formed. Austria opted to stay out, but smaller states joined, creating a single inland market that replaced a whole range of customs, currencies, and controls.

The state of Brandenburg-Prussia expanded its power during the second half of the 19th century under the leadership of its prime minister, Otto von Bismarck. The brief German-Danish War of 1864 gained Schleswig and Holstein for Prussia and Austria. In 1866, Prussia defeated Austria to secure these lands after a dispute over their control, emerging as the most powerful state in Germany.

Before 1850, Germany lagged far behind the leaders in industrial development, Britain, France, and Belgium. By mid-century, the German states were catching up and by 1900, Germany had become a world leader in industrialization.

King William I of Prussia proclaimed as kaiser in the Hall of Mirrors in Versailles.

Prussia, subsequently, dissolved the German Confederation and replaced it with the North German Federation. Bismarck was chosen chancellor of this federation and, in 1870, a short, victorious war with France added the provinces of Alsace and Lorraine. The southern German states later joined their northern neighbors, forming the German empire, or *Reich* (RIKE). On January 18, 1871, King William I of Prussia became the kaiser, or German emperor, of an empire of 25 states. During 1871, the unified nation state of the German Empire was assigned an official capital. Prussia was the dominant part of the unified Germany and its capital, Berlin, was chosen as the capital of the nation, remaining so until the end of World War II.

WORLD WAR I

The year 1918 was the year of the deadly Spanish flu pandemic, which struck hard at a German population weakened by years of malnutrition.

Longing to have overseas colonies like those of Britain and France, Germany rebuilt its navy. As Germany's military was already the most powerful in Europe, the country's colonial ambitions troubled its neighbors. In 1907, Britain, France, and Russia formed an alliance called the Triple Entente.

War was sparked by the assassination of Archduke Franz Ferdinand, the heir to the Austrian throne, in Serbia in June 1914. Austria invaded Serbia with German support, while Russia, supported by France, sided with Serbia. Germany declared war on France, invading Belgium in order to destroy French defenses. Britain entered the war in defense of Belgium.

World War I turned out to be the worst war Europe had ever seen. Fighting in the trenches in northeastern France lasted for four years, with terrible casualties on both sides. The United States' entry into the war in 1917 helped turn the tide against Germany and its allies.

Following a cease-fire, a treaty was signed, and World War I ended in November 1918. Kaiser William II gave up his throne and fled.

RESULTS OF WORLD WAR I The Treaty of Versailles held Germany and its allies fully responsible for the war. The victors imposed reparations (war payments) and tried to prevent a future rise of the German military.

In the war and subsequent peace, Germany lost 27,000 square miles (70,000 square km) of territory, 7.2 million people, 15 percent of its farming output, 10 percent of its manufacturing capacity, 75 percent of its iron-ore production, and all its overseas colonies. East and West Prussia were separated to allow Poland access to the Baltic Sea, and Danzig (now Gdansk in Poland) was declared a free city. Alsace-Lorraine went to France, which also occupied the coal-rich Saarland area. Three million ethnic Germans were left outside German territory.

From left to right: Field Marshall Paul von Hindenburg, Kaiser William II, and General Erich Ludendorff in the German headquarters planning an assault against the Allies during World War I. Hindenburg later became the president of Germany.

The eviction of an unemployed family in Berlin during the Great Depression.

THE WEIMAR REPUBLIC

Following Germany's devastating military defeat, a provisional government tasked with drafting a democratic constitution for the new German republic was set up in the city of Weimar. Well-meaning but ultimately unconvincing Social Democrat politicians attempted to put the country back on its feet, but the loss of Alsace-Lorraine to France and the heavy reparations burden crippled the country economically. In 1923, Germany could not pay its reparations, which led France to occupy the Ruhr coalfields to extract its own form of compensation.

Morale dropped drastically, and inflation reached astronomic proportions, virtually leading the country into a barter economy where goods were exchanged. The U.S. stock market crash of 1929 and the Great Depression that followed further hurt the German economy, leaving Germany with 7 million unemployed. These harsh socio-economic conditions led to the rise of extremist groups.

During the Holocaust, millions of Jews, Poles, Romanies, and Slavs in Germany and German-occupied areas were systematically killed.

THE HITLER YEARS

The National Socialist Party, or the Nazis, an extreme right-wing organization led by Adolf Hitler, opposed communism and blamed Jewish bankers and financiers, as well as France's hostile reparations demands, for Germany's plight. Support for the Nazis grew, and by 1932 they had become the strongest party in parliament.

On January 30, 1933, Hitler was appointed chancellor by President Paul von Hindenburg. In 1934 Hindenburg died, and Hitler proclaimed himself leader, or führer, with almost absolute powers. In 1935 the Saarland voted to return to Germany, and the following year Hitler defied the Versailles peace terms by remilitarizing the Rhine area. This policy had gained popularity for the Nazi party among the German people, as desperately needed jobs were created in arms manufacturing and highway construction.

Hitler's insane vision of German racial supremacy began to take shape. He sought to "purify" the Aryan race by selective genetic breeding and the destruction of the Jews. German Jews were arrested and their businesses destroyed. During the early 1940s, the Nazis sent millions of Jews from Germany and Poland to concentration camps to be tortured and killed.

WORLD WAR II Hitler's efforts to create a mighty German state began in 1938 with the annexation of Austria, followed by parts of Czechoslovakia. On September 1, 1939, World War II began when Germany invaded Poland. Britain and France, Poland's allies, immediately declared war on Germany. Poland was defeated, and former Prussian lands were "returned" to Germany. Hitler's armies conquered Denmark and Norway, followed by Belgium, the Netherlands, France, Yugoslavia, and Greece. In 1940 Germany, Japan, and Italy formed a fascist alliance. In 1941 Hitler turned against his former ally, the Soviet Union, and invaded Russia. When Japan attacked Pearl Harbor in December 1941, Germany declared war on the United States.

In late 1942 the German armies suffered terrible losses in the Soviet Union and North Africa. In 1943, Allied troops from the United States and Britain, which had formed a military alliance, defeated Italy. Allied troops landed in France in 1944 and swept into Germany. From the east, Soviet armies drove to Berlin. On April 30, 1945, surrounded on all sides, Hitler committed suicide and Germany surrendered.

Adolf Hitler of the Nazi party saluting the crowds during his leadership.

After the U.S. offered the Marshall Plan to Eastern and Western European countries, Eastern countries rejected it on the advice of the Soviet Union. West Germany then introduced its radical postwar currency reform in 1948. This was followed by Soviet leader Josef Stalin attempting to win the whole city for the Communist East by imposing a blockade.

In June 1948 the Soviet Union blockaded the western part of Berlin, closing all land corridors and railway access to the city from the west. Because food, fuel, and raw materials needed in the factories were transported from the western side of the country, the blockade left Berliners without access to basic supplies.

The blockade lasted 10 months, from June 1948 to May 1949. The gamble failed because the Western Allied powers began a round-the-clock airlift into the city. Western planes flew 120,000 flights into West Berlin, bringing 1.5 million tons of food, medical supplies, and other essentials to supply the 2 million inhabitants. Eventually Stalin realized that he would not succeed in overtaking the city in this manner, so he ordered the blockade to be lifted.

POSTWAR GERMANY

Immediately after its surrender, Germany was demilitarized and divided into four administrative zones by France, Britain, the United States, and the Soviet Union. An agreement on how to govern Germany was reached in late 1945. Britain, France, and the United States would govern the western two-thirds of Germany, and the Soviet Union would govern the eastern third. Within the Soviet zone lay the capital, Berlin, which was also divided into four administrative zones. All of northeastern Prussia went to the Soviet Union and all German territories east of the Oder River were under Polish control. As a result about 9.5 million Germans living in the eastern regions were expelled and forced to immigrate to West Germany. As many as 1 million people may have died on the way.

With the start of the Cold War between the East and the West, the Allies' concerns shifted from German reconstruction to stopping the spread of communism. In 1948 the western zones were turned into the Federal Republic of Germany. The following year, Konrad Adenauer was appointed its first chancellor. This division between the communist and non-communist controlled sections of Germany and Berlin was intended to be temporary but remained until 1990. In 1949 the Soviet-occupied zone was renamed the Democratic Republic of Germany.

West Germany remained occupied and only attained self-rule in 1955. East Germans came under the rule of the Socialist Unity Party (SED), or the East German Communist Party, led by Walter Ulbricht.

Germans demonstrating against the construction of the Berlin Wall in 1961.

EAST-WEST GERMAN RELATIONS

With the introduction of communist principles, the redistribution of land and wealth, and the Soviet Union's crippling reparations demands, thousands of East Germans left for the wealthier West. Aside from economic reasons, many people left to join family members on the other side of the new border. In June 1953 a revolt in East Berlin and other East German towns was put down by Soviet troops. The 854-mile (1,375-km) border between East and West Germany was fortified to become a guarded barrier, which became known as the Iron Curtain. In 1961 the Berlin Wall was built.

During the 1960s, at the height of the Cold War, there was little communication between the two Germanys. Later that decade, Chancellor Willy Brandt of West Germany started *Ostpolitik* (OST-poll-ee-teek), a program of meeting with the East German government to improve relations between East and West Germany. A few years later, a treaty was signed. West German citizens were allowed to visit relatives in the East for limited periods, but East Germans were not allowed to travel to the West.

People from East and West Berlin gathering at Brandenburg Gate to climb and celebrate the fall of the Berlin Wall, and reunification of the country.

REUNIFICATION

The West German constitution had always regarded the division of Germany as temporary and provided for the reunification of the country. West Germany always welcomed as citizens all East German refugees who did manage the incredibly difficult passage across the border.

When Mikhail Gorbachev started his policy of glasnost, translated as openness, in the Soviet Union in the late 1980s, the gradual decrease of Soviet control over East Germany and Eastern Europe led to peaceful revolutions.

In May 1989, East Germans on vacation in Hungary took advantage of the country's newly opened borders and crossed via Austria into West Germany. Other East Germans sought refuge at West German embassies in Czechoslovakia and Poland. Later that year, the first steps toward reunification were taken when East German travel restrictions were lifted. A visit to East Germany by Gorbachev in October 1989 made it clear that Soviet troops would no longer support the country. Barely a month later, the Berlin Wall was torn down. Talks on reunification between the East and West German governments progressed rapidly, and a treaty of unification was signed on October 3, 1990.

The first full democratic parliamentary elections, in which East and West Germans voted together as one country, took place two months later. Helmut Kohl was elected chancellor of a reunified Germany.

The Social Democratic Party of Germany (SPD) in coalition with the Greens won the elections of 1998. SPD leader Gerhard Schröder positioned himself as a centrist Third Way candidate in the mold of Britain's Tony Blair and America's Bill Clinton. Schröder, in March 2003, reversed his position and proposed a significant downsizing of the welfare state, known as Agenda 2010. He had enough support to overcome opposition from the trade unions and the SPD's left wing.

As of 2013, for eight consecutive years Germany was ruled by a grand coalition led by Angela Merkel of the Christian Democratic Union (CDU) as chancellor. Along with France, Germany has played a leading role in the European Union (EU). Germany, especially under Chancellor Kohl, was one of the main supporters of admitting many East European countries to the EU. Germany is at the forefront of European states seeking to exploit the momentum of monetary union to advance the creation of a more unified and capable European political, defense, and security apparatus.

INTERNET LINKS

www.germanculture.com.ua/library/history/bl_german_history.htm

A comprehensive website on German history and culture.

http://germanhistorydocs.ghi-dc.org/Index.cfm?language=english

An excellent collection of primary source materials on German history from 1500 to the present, consisting mainly of documents, images, and maps.

http://www.historyworld.net/wrldhis/PlainTextHistories. asp?historyid=ac62

Offers a linear approach toward the history of Germany.

West Germany was rapidly restored to independence by the Allies after World War II. It joined the North Atlantic Treaty Organization (NATO) in the 1950s, reforming its army in 1956. In 1963, United States president John F. Kennedy visited the country to develop close relations and summed up his feelings during a visit to Berlin: *"Ich bin ein Berliner!"* ("I am a Berliner!")

GOVERNMENT

The rebuilt Reichstag in Berlin boasts an impressive crystal dome, which is meant to represent the transparency of German politics.

3

GERMANY HAS a federal, decentralized system of government, in which each state, or *Land* (LAHND), has the right to govern its citizens independently from the central government. Each state has its own constitution, although its regulations must fall within the guidelines set forth in the Basic Law, Germany's set of governing laws established in 1949.

Germany is a parliamentary democracy governed under the constitution of 1949, which became the constitution of a united Germany in 1990.

FEDERAL GOVERNMENT

The federal style of the German government has its roots in the theories of 15th-century Dutch Calvinist political thinker Johannes Althusius. He advocated the right of every social group to provide for the well-being of its members. In its modern-day form, a federal government allows a wide application of democratic principles on the local and national level.

The federal system allows for many checks and balances. For example, the head of the German government, the federal chancellor, is in charge of the armed forces only in times of war; during peacetime, the army is under the control of the federal minister of defense.

There are two houses of government in Germany: the Bundestag, which consists of 620 members elected by citizens every four years, who in turn elects the federal chancellor; and the Bundesrat, made up of nominees from the state governments who represent the varied interests of the states.

Voting is not compulsory, but anyone over the age of 18 has the right to vote. The German president is the head of state. The president officially appoints the federal chancellor once the latter is elected by the Bundestag. The duties of the federal president are largely representative and ceremonial. He is not a member of the government. The president is elected every five years by the Federal Assembly, a special body convened only for this purpose. This selective group consists of the entire Bundestag and an equal number of state delegates.

In June 1991 the German parliament voted to move the Bundestag from its premises in Bonn to Berlin. In September 1999 the parliament held its inaugural session in the Reichstag in Berlin. The Bundesrat has also moved to a newly renovated historical building in Berlin. The federal government is responsible for defense, foreign policy, transportation, postal services, currency, trade tariffs, and issuing passports. It shares duties with the state governments for civil and criminal law enforcement, labor law, road traffic, and economic matters, having the right to legislate when necessary to ensure uniform laws for the whole country. Income from taxes is divided between the federal and state governments.

As of March 2012, the Bundeswehr (Germany's military) employs 183,000 professional soldiers and has 17,000 volunteers. It is a purely defensive force, meaning that it exists for the protection of the German nation and is not allowed to start an attack unless directly provoked. Compulsory conscription in Germany was suspended on July 1, 2011, part of plans to reduce the size of the German postwar military that stood at 240,000 conscripted soldiers to a professional army signed up for a fixed period of service. Voluntary basic training is still an option, which can last between 12 and 23 months and is open to both men and women. Between 7,000 and 15,000 volunteers are expected each year. Some mourn the passing of a long-standing tradition and a great social leveler, while others say the reform is long overdue.

STATE GOVERNMENTS

Each of the states has its own elected parliament, called Landesrat. As with the federal government, voting is optional, and all citizens over 18 years of age have the right to vote.

The state governments are responsible for health care, education policies, broadcasting, and cultural affairs. They make and administer local laws and environmental protection measures, run their own police forces, and enforce traffic regulations and federal laws.

The local governments in turn look after the towns, communities, and counties. Those serving in Mayoral positions are well paid in order to attract talented individuls.

The local authorities collect certain taxes and share in others, although each state grants them additional revenues to keep solvent. Revenue problems frequently arise at the state level. For instance, the city-state of Hamburg has high property taxes. People who live just outside its borders and commute pay lower rates to the state, which decreases Hamburg's revenue.

A political rally held by the Pirate party in Germany.

POLITICAL PARTIES

Germany has a multiparty system with two major parties, the Social Democratic Party of Germany (SPD) and the Christian Democratic Union (CDU), with its sister party, the Christian Social Union (CSU) in the same parliamentary group, also known as CDU/CSU or the Union. Germany also has four minor parties: the Free Democratic Party (FDP), the Left, the Pirates (Piratenpartei), and Alliance '90/the Greens (Bündnis '90/Die Grünen). The federal government of Germany usually consists of a coalition of a major and a minor party, most typically CDU/CSU and FDP, or an alliance of the SPD and Greens.

There are various smaller political parties, generally more powerful at the state than federal level. But their political power is hampered by a law that states that only parties that have gained 5 percent or more of the votes in an election can send representatives to the Bundestag, a check that has so far stopped extreme right- and left-wing parties from gaining seats.

THE LEGAL SYSTEM

Germany has a highly regulated society. Identity cards are issued to German citizens by local registration offices (although today they are produced

The Bundesrat has its seat at the former Prussian House of Lords in Berlin.

In 1983 the Green Party, which evolved from a radical environmental protection movement, won its first seats in the Bundestag. It has won seats in all federal and many state parliaments since. The party campaigns on nuclear issues, industrial pollution, saving the natural heritage, and pacifism. Its social and welfare programs include the belief that each individual should receive an income, whether or not he or she has a job. The party has inspired other groups in Europe and has succeeded in bringing environmental issues into the political scene. Alliance '90 is an alliance of three noncommunist political groups in East Germany. It merged with the German Green Party in 1993 to form Alliance '90/the Greens. In the 2009 federal elections,

Alliance '90/the Greens won 10.7 percent of the votes and 68 of 620 seats in the Bundestag. In 2011 the Greens made large gains in Rhineland-Palatinate and Baden-Württemberg.

centrally by the federal printer, Bundesdruckerei, in Berlin). Citizens must carry identification cards or papers and drive with their license and insurance documents, and they can be fined for crossing the road where there is no pedestrian crossing.

The Basic Law lays out numerous rules to protect democracy and freedom of speech and guarantees a catalog of human rights that includes the protection of political refugees. There is no death penalty in Germany.

There are six types of courts: the ordinary court for criminal and civil cases; the labor court for labor relations; the administrative court for all administrative laws; the social court for social programs; the fiscal court for tax matters; and the federal constitutional court, which is the highest court of appeal as well as a constitutional and legislative body.

REUNIFICATION Vast differences between the former East Germany and West Germany (for example, in lifestyle, wealth, and political beliefs) remain, and it is therefore still common to speak of eastern and western Germany distinctly. The Eastern German economy has struggled since unification, and large subsidies are still transferred from west to east. The former East Germany area has often been compared to that of the underdeveloped southern Italy and the Southern United States during reconstruction after the American Civil War. While the East German economy has recovered recently, the differences between East and West remain constant.

German unity has been a shaky marriage. Many Easterners have endured change, hardship, upheaval, and other negative developments, sometimes even being evicted from houses that people who fled during the Cold War returned to reclaim. Many are still struggling to come to terms with life in reunited Germany, and are nostalgic about life in East Germany, to the great irritation of Western Germans who have helped pay €1.6 trillion ($2.1 trillion) to rebuild the East.

Reasons for their disenchantment can be seen everywhere: the Eastern population has shrunk by about 2 million, unemployment soared upon reunification, and young people moved away in droves. Former East Germany is also now largely devoid of industry.

The Basic Law for the Federal Republic of Germany is the constitution of Germany. It was first signed into law in former West Germany on May 23, 1949. Some changes were made to the law in 1990, mostly pertaining to reunification. Additional modifications to the Basic Law were made in 1994, 2002, and 2006.

INTERNET LINKS

www.bundesregierung.de/Webs/Breg/EN/Homepage/_node.html

The home page of the German federal government, where press statements and information on government initiatives are available.

www.tatsachen-ueber-deutschland.de/en/political-system/main-content-04/the-federal-structure.html

Everything you could possibly want to know about how Germany is governed.

www.rogerdarlington.me.uk/Germanpoliticalsystem.html

A concise summary of the German political system.

ECONOMY

The landmark BMW Tower in Munich is the world headquarters for the Bavarian automaker.

4

S INCE THE AGE OF industrialization, Germany has been a driver, innovator, and beneficiary of an increasingly globalized economy. Germany is Europe's largest economy and the fourth largest economy in the world. It is a world leader in technologically advanced production of iron, steel, coal, cement, chemicals, machinery, vehicles, machine tools, electronics, food and beverages, shipbuilding, and textiles.

The service sector contributed around 70.6 percent of the total gross domestic product (GDP), industry 28.6 percent, and agriculture 0.8 percent in 2012. Germany is the world's leading producer of wind turbines and solar power technology. Some of the largest annual international trade fairs and congresses are held in German cities, such as Hannover, Frankfurt, and Berlin. Of the Fortune Global 500, the world's 500 largest publicly traded companies measured by revenue, 37 are headquartered in Germany.

POSTWAR ECONOMIC MIRACLE

More than half of West Germany's industrial capacity was destroyed during World War II, and an additional 5 percent was taken from existing capital and foreign assets as part of war payments. In East Germany,

With a Gross Domestic Product (GDP) of $3.1 trillion, Germany is the largest national economy in Europe, followed by France. However, Germany's real GDP growth has been dampened by the euro-zone sovereign debt crisis.

the Soviet Union moved currency production, and sometimes entire plants, to the USSR.

During the 1950s, West Germany experienced fantastic economic growth. The *Wirtschaftswunder* (VIRT-shafts-voon-der), or economic miracle, was largely the result of the hard work and determination of the German people to succeed. The country reached economic stability by 1953 and full employment by 1959. Industrial production rose by 130 percent in the late 1950s.

Other factors contributed to this success. The Marshall Plan, started by the United States, provided economic aid. A bold currency reform attacked inflation. Price and wage controls were abolished, and a sensible industrial-relations policy was achieved. The Korean War in the 1950s increased demand for manufactured goods.

INFRASTRUCTURE AND COMMUNICATIONS

Present-day Germany has a highly effective infrastructure and communications system. The federal government owns and subsidizes the postal services. With its central position in Europe, Germany is an important transportation hub. This is reflected in its dense and modern transportation networks. The extensive motorway, or autobahn, network ranks third in the world in length and features a lack of speed limits on the majority of its roads.

Germany has established a polycentric network of high-speed trains. The Intercity-Express, or ICE, serves major German cities as well as destinations in neighboring countries. The maximum speed varies between 100 mph and 185 mph (161 kph—298 kph). Connections are offered at 30-minute, hourly, or two-hourly intervals.

Germany also has an extensive network of inland waterways—rivers and canals—linking the industrial towns of the Rhine River with the Baltic ports and the rest of the European market. Twenty-five percent of its manufactured and agricultural goods are transported on water, of which 70 percent go through the Rhine River. The Nord-Ostsee Canal across the state of Schleswig-Holstein is a busy route for goods traveling between the Baltic Sea and North Sea.

Germany's largest airline is former national carrier Lufthansa, which was privatized in the 1990s. The group includes domestic subsidiaries Lufthansa Cityline and Eurowings, which operate as Lufthansa Regional, as well as independently operating low-cost subsidiary Germanwings.

The telecommunications system in Germany is highly developed. The German telecommunications market has been fully liberalized since January 1, 1998. As a result of intensive capital expense since reunification, the outdated telecommunications infrastructure of former East Germany has been upgraded.

A vegetable field with savoy cabbage and brussels sprouts in Münsterland, North Rhine-Westphalia.

INDUSTRIES

As it lacks significant natural resources, Germany must import most of its raw materials and energy sources. It does, however, have profitable bituminous and brown coal (lignite) deposits in the Ruhr and Saar valleys. Germany's steel industry is concentrated near these areas. The country also has small amounts of iron ore, petroleum, and natural gas.

Industry and construction accounted for 28.6 percent of GDP and employed 24.6 percent of the workforce in 2012. Germany benefits from having a highly skilled labor force and is an important world exporter of machinery, vehicles, chemicals, and household equipment.

AGRICULTURE

Agriculture, forestry, and mining accounted for only 1 percent of Germany's 2012 GDP and employed only 1.6 percent of the population, down from 4 percent in 1991. Nonetheless, Germany is able to cover 90 percent of its nutritional needs with domestic production. Germany is the third

Currently six German companies dominate the automotive industry in the country: Volkswagen, BMW, Mercedes-Benz, Porsche, Opel, and Ford-Werke GmbH.

THE GERMAN CAR INDUSTRY

With the manufacture of 5.2 million vehicles in 2009, Germany was the world's fourth-largest producer of automobiles, after the United States, China, and Japan, and the largest exporter. German automotive companies enjoy an extremely strong position in the so-called premium segment, with a combined world market share of about 90 percent. The greatest success of the German car industry has been in the area of expensive high-performance vehicles.

Probably the most famous luxury car in the world today, the Mercedes-Benz had its beginnings in Germany. A man named Gottlieb Daimler invented the gasoline engine in the 1880s in the city of Stuttgart, while another, Karl Benz, was starting similar developments some 80 miles (129 km) away in Mannheim. Emil Jellinek, a diplomat and a major investor in Daimler's firm, suggested that Daimler's new line of cars, which sported a four-cylinder engine, be named after Jellinek's daughter Mercedes. Jellinek feared that the German-sounding Daimler name would not appeal to the French. In 1901 Daimler sold the first Mercedes car. Although the Daimler and Benz companies only fully merged in 1960, Mercedes-Benz has been a household name around the world for decades. In 1998 the biggest merger of two industrial companies in history took place when Daimler-Benz joined American car manufacturer Chrysler to form DaimlerChrysler.

Another famous German car company, Bayerische Motoren Werke, more commonly known as BMW, made aircraft engines during World War I and then expanded into motorcycles and sports cars. But in the 1950s, its future was uncertain until the main shareholders, the Quandt family, took over and made it the automobile power that it is today.

The product of another German car company rivals that of Daimler-Benz for the title of the most famous German car in the world. In 1938, Volkswagen (meaning "People's Car") started mass production of an automobile designed in 1936 by an Austrian named Ferdinand Porsche: the "Beetle." The company remained fully nationalized until 1961, but its sales started to slip as Germans became wealthier and could afford luxury cars. To meet this challenge, Volkswagen developed the "yuppie car" of the 1980s, the best-selling Volkswagen Golf. These are all in production at the Volkswagen car factory at Wolfsburg (below).

Volkswagen has ties with two other famous car companies. First, the company owns Audi, producer of a popular luxury car. Second, when Ferdinand Porsche left Volkswagen in the 1950s, he started his own car company. Sports-car lovers admired the sleek design of Porsche. In 2001, 50 percent of Porsche's sales were to the United States. The company is still run by the Porsche family.

In contrast with West Germany's successful car industry, the former East German car company Trabant closed down shortly after German reunification, when faced with strong competition from other, more-established carmakers. As a result, 1 million jobs were lost.

largest agricultural producer in the European Union, after France and Italy. Germany's principal agricultural products are potatoes, wheat, barley, sugar beets, fruit, cabbages, cattle, pigs, and poultry.

Despite the country's high level of industrialization, almost one-third of Germany's territory is covered by forest. The forestry industry provides for only about two-thirds of domestic consumption of wood and wood products, so Germany is a net importer of these items.

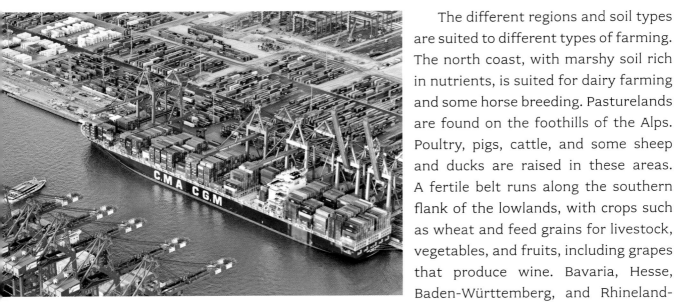

The different regions and soil types are suited to different types of farming. The north coast, with marshy soil rich in nutrients, is suited for dairy farming and some horse breeding. Pasturelands are found on the foothills of the Alps. Poultry, pigs, cattle, and some sheep and ducks are raised in these areas. A fertile belt runs along the southern flank of the lowlands, with crops such as wheat and feed grains for livestock, vegetables, and fruits, including grapes that produce wine. Bavaria, Hesse, Baden-Württemberg, and Rhineland-Palatinate have forestry farming.

A container ship loading in the commercial port of Hamburg.

Farming in Germany is regulated by the Common Agricultural Policy of the European Union, which at first encouraged overproduction of certain grain crops but is now penalizing overproduction to prevent farm prices from falling further. Fishing in the North Sea is also governed by numerous regulations.

GERMANY AND EUROPE

While many other countries had been booming in the first years of the 21st century, Germany was dubbed the "Sick Man of Europe" as it struggled to cope with the ongoing economic effects of reunification. In 2005 unemployment reached a peak of 12.5 percent, crucially exceeding the 5 million mark. This led the government to push through a wide-ranging program of belt-tightening reforms. At the same time Germany, as a leading exporter, began to profit from the overall high growth of the world economy. But when, in 2008, the global economy fell into recession, so did Germany. In January 2009 the German government under Angela Merkel approved a €50 billion ($70 billion) economic stimulus plan to protect several sectors from a downturn and a subsequent rise in unemployment rates. Germany had emerged from its recession by the third quarter of 2009, thanks to rebounding manufacturing

Germany is the world's biggest exporter, with exports accounting for more than one-third of national output in 2012.

orders and exports—primarily from outside the eurozone—and relatively steady consumer demand. The year 2011 was a record-breaking one for the German economy. German companies exported goods worth more than €1 trillion ($1.3 trillion), the highest figure in history. The number of people employed rose to 41.6 million, the highest recorded figure. Germany's GDP (real growth rate) was 3.1 percent in 2011. By 2012 the real growth rate was 0.7 percent.

Ever since 2008, the European Union has been struggling with a debt crisis, and although most of the member countries were coping with sky-high unemployment, Germany has emerged relatively unscathed. As of May 2012 it had an unemployment rate of just 6.7 percent. Chancellor Merkel advocates austerity measures for the countries facing the worst of the debt crisis, such as Greece, Ireland, and Portugal, but opinion in Europe is strong that it is a matter of time before Germany has to step in to bail out the euro currency and member countries in the eurozone. Countries such as Belgium, Italy, Spain, and France are also trying to stave off the effects of their burgeoning debt.

BANKING AND FINANCE

All three of the major German banks, Deutsche Bank, Commerzbank, and Dresdner Bank, were founded in the 1870s. Frankfurt remains the banking center of Germany and an international center of finance. The Frankfurt Stock Exchange (Deutsche Börse) offers the lowest capital costs among the world's leading stock exchanges. Frankfurt was chosen as the site for the EU's European Central Bank. Other exchanges can be found in Bremen, Düsseldorf, Hamburg, Munich, Hannover, Stuttgart, and Berlin.

The gleaming Deutsche Bank AG Twin Towers in Frankfurt, Hesse.

EAST AND WEST DISPARITIES

The economic challenges brought about by reunification have been great. Industries and businesses in the former East have not been able to remain competitive under capitalism, and many have closed. West German managerial skills, on the other hand, have saved some industries.

A government organization, the Treuhandanstalt, or Trust Agency, was set up to transform the entire East German economy into a free-market economy. By 1994 the agency had turned over approximately 14,000 formerly state-owned enterprises—98 percent of those entrusted to it—into private hands. Hundreds of thousands of new businesses have opened, and both West German and foreign firms, led by giants such as Siemens and General Motors, have set up shop in the former East Germany. In 1998 the eastern states were home to 520,000 small and mid-size businesses with a total of 3.2 million employees. The number of self-employed Easterners jumped in about 10 years from 30,000 to 240,000.

THE PROBLEMS OF REUNIFICATION The former East Germany had huge infrastructure costs to bear, as almost all its housing and commercial buildings were rundown and in need of repair. Public and private investment has done much to bring the East's basic infrastructure up to par with that of the West. Since 1990 more than a half-million housing units have been built and 3.5 million existing residences have been renovated. Close to 7,000 miles (11,265 km) of roads and 3,000 miles (4,828 km) of rail lines have been rebuilt or newly constructed. The telecommunications system was replaced and now ranks among the most advanced in the world.

An aerial view of the Kamener Kreuz motorway junction in North Rhine-Westphalia. It lies between the towns of Kamen and Bergkamen in the west and the city of Hamm and the municipality Bönen in the east.

WORKING LIFE

Germany has a powerful set of labor laws protecting workers' rights. Laborers have a real say in the running of their workplaces by having a system of worker participation in management. Companies employing more than 2,000 people have an *Aufsichtsrat* (OWF-sikts-raht), a council composed of delegates from workers and management. Firms with more than five employees must have a *Betriebsrat* (Bye-TREEBS-raht), a workers' council. These councils are consulted on matters of recruitment, dismissals, unemployment, and new technology. During the 1930s the labor movement was divided into more than 200 groups, making resistance to Nazism impossible. Today there are seven unions within the Deutscher Gewerkschaftsbund, the Confederation of German Trade Unions. However, with the prolonged recession and the debt crisis in Europe, union membership has dropped to less than 20 percent of the workforce. Germans are now willing to negotiate and accept less favorable working conditions in order to save their jobs.

Trade unions have a long history in Germany, reaching back to the German revolution in 1848, and still play an important role in the German economy and society.

INTERNET LINKS

www.econlib.org/library/Enc/GermanEconomicMiracle.html

A compelling account of how Germany rose from postwar shambles to the economic miracle that it is today. Links to definitions of economic terms are provided.

www.economist.com/topics/german-economy

A collection of thoughtful articles on the German economy and the role Germany is playing in the European Union.

www.spiegel.de/international/topic/german_economy/

Numerous reports about the German economy, the European Union, and trends.

ENVIRONMENT

A view of the Elbe River and the Wartturm rocks from the spectacular Bastei rock formation in the Saxon Switzerland National Park in Dresden.

ENVIRONMENTAL ISSUES ARE extremely important in Germany. Germans make a conscious effort to protect the environment. This caring attitude is the result of long-standing active public concern and participation, as well as progressive government policies and legislation that place strict limits on all forms of noise, water, air, and ground pollution.

Pollution prevention is only one facet of Germany's comprehensive approach to environmental conservation. The country is also committed to ensuring that recycling and the protection of natural resources are maximized in all spheres of human activity. This goal is achieved by several means—preventing pollution from entering the environment, promoting energy efficiency in the use of natural resources in the home and industry, and halting and reversing the depletion of land and natural resources. As stated in Germany's Basic Law, the aim of environmental policies is to protect vital natural resources for future generations.

As a result, the country is a leading producer of environmental technology and services aimed not only at eliminating pollution but also at developing renewable energy and protecting natural resources and the environment. This technical expertise is backed by some of Europe's most environmentally aware citizens, who are actively involved in protecting their natural heritage and scenic countryside.

A number of cities
in Germany have
been classified
as low-emission
zones, and only
vehicles that have
been certified as
"low emitters" of
pollution may enter
these zones.

ENVIRONMENTAL LEGISLATION

Between 1990 and 2005, Germany's greenhouse-gas emissions declined 18 percent. In the same period, those of the United States increased 16 percent. The government has left little to chance. An eco-tax on fuel discourages petroleum use. Laws push waste reduction and recycling, producers must pay to deal with packaging they create. Subsidies encourage people to retrofit their homes with solar panels.

RENEWABLE ENERGY RESOURCES LAW

Without prescribing any specific action, this law subsidizes citizens who produce their own energy from renewable sources and allows them to sell surplus back to the electricity grid. The subsidies have meant that the production of renewable energy has ramped up quickly. The Environment Ministry estimates that more than 14 percent of the country's electricity now comes from renewable sources.

AIR POLLUTION

As one of the world's leading industrialized nations, Germany has come to terms with the impact that its heavy industrial activity and road traffic have had on the natural environment. Pollutants have caused great damage to Germany's atmosphere. Acid rain, which results from air pollution, eats away at the country's forests and lakes, destroying the natural habitat of wildlife. Acid rain also damages Germany's numerous historic buildings and town centers.

A far-reaching clean air program has been implemented, targeting air pollution at its source. Measures have been taken to implement laws requiring car drivers, power stations, heavy industrial plants, and other polluting buildings or machinery to install catalytic converters, devices to treat exhaust gases before they are released into the air.

The government aims to reduce pollutants from traffic by banning the use of leaded gasoline and introducing tighter emissions standards for all classes of vehicles, regardless of whether they are road users, which means that aircraft are also affected. There is a concerted effort toward the creation of environmentally sustainable transportation by using new technology and educating the public on viable alternatives to fossil fuels.

The most visible signs of this changing mentality are probably the increasing appearance of buses that run on natural gas in urban centers across the country, as well as the promotion of bicycles as a healthy form of transportation on congested city roads.

Germany has worked to persuade its European partners to follow its lead in implementing creative environmental programs and has brought about the successful adoption of a standardized European Union policy for clean fuels.

NOISE AND WATER POLLUTION

Germany has been active in reducing noise pollution across the country through the adoption and enforcement of strict noise-control measures, especially in urban residential areas. The government has taken the first step by reducing traffic as well as controlling noise from cars and other vehicles. The Blue Angel "environment friendly" label, in use since 1977, has helped to raise awareness of all pollution issues, including noise, among the general public. This label, although not legally binding, is sought after by manufacturers because of the sales boost it gives a product that is recognized as environmentally friendly.

Water-pollution issues are often international, as rivers cross borders. Germany has been working closely with its neighbors to remedy water pollution and has contributed handsomely to cleanup measures abroad. Germany and its neighbors have signed cooperation agreements concerning the protection of the Danube, Oder, and Elbe rivers.

Levels of water pollution from Germany's industrial centers have also declined during the past decade as a result of tougher legislation on industrial wastewater disposal. The levels of lead in the Rhine River have decreased by half. Nitrate levels in the waterways caused by runoffs of agricultural chemicals have fallen as well.

Germany's efforts do not aim simply to reduce the existing level of water pollution but also to remedy past abuses to the environment and rehabilitate once-choked waterways into clean, ecologically viable habitats for people and wildlife alike.

German citizens must separate and dispose of garbage according to strict regulations. Color-coded bins are used for collecting different types of recyclable waste.

FLOOD PREVENTION

Disastrous floods have hit Germany in recent years. On January 10, 2011, melting snow and rising temperatures caused by global warming resulted in the Rhine and Mosel rivers bursting their banks. This affected Cologne, North Rhine-Westphalia, Hesse, Saxony-Anhalt, Baden-Württemberg, and Bavaria.

The government has put a great deal of effort into alleviating the effects—both human and economic—of past floods and is working to prevent similar catastrophes from recurring. Measures to remedy the effects of floods, beyond the existing work to ensure clear paths for Germany's waterways, have included identifying and shielding damage-prone floodplains as well as improving area capabilities for retention and absorption of precipitation.

RECYCLING

Germany takes the world lead in recycling. In 2009, Germans recycled 48 percent of municipal waste and composted an additional 18 percent. The widespread use of glass instead of plastic containers and the rapid growth of comprehensive recycling facilities bear testimony to the determination and commitment the government has put into this initiative, as well as to the efficiency with which it has implemented the program nationwide. The myriad recycling bins available also attest to how widely recycling is practiced.

The country's recycling-friendly Green Dot scheme is known worldwide, and thanks to Germany's phenomenal export success, consumer items bearing the scheme's logo can be seen on supermarket shelves around the globe. The Green Dot "polluter pays" campaign, by which producers must ensure the proper disposal of the packaging of their products, has recently been joined by recycling requirements for end users, requiring them to pay a deposit on various types of containers, refundable on the return of these to designated outlets.

AN END TO NUCLEAR POWER

Nuclear power in Germany accounted for 23 percent of national electricity consumption, before the permanent shutdown of eight plants in March 2011. Six of these plants had been temporarily shut down for testing, and two more had been offline for a few years with technical problems. On May 30, 2011, Germany formally announced plans to abandon nuclear energy completely within 11 years, with its nine remaining plants shut down by 2022. Chancellor Angela Merkel said the phaseout of plants, previously scheduled to go offline as late as 2036, would give Germany a competitive advantage in the renewable-energy era.

Wind and solar farms in Südergellersen, Lower Saxony.

THE WAY FORWARD

Across Germany, it is common to see houses with solar-photovoltaic panels on their south-facing roofs. Germans are now building giant offshore wind farms in the North Sea. The windmills are hundreds of feet tall, with blades the length of football fields. Germany's emphasis on renewable energy has done more than help the country meet its climate-change goals. It has been an economic success too. There are now nearly 250,000 Germans employed in the renewable-energy sector, and renewable-energy exports have boomed. Environmentalism is deeply embedded throughout German politics. As German industries discovered, they could thrive despite tough environmental regulations, and indeed develop export markets for green technologies. Hence a broad consensus on the benefits of going green has emerged nationwide.

NATIONAL PARKS AND RESERVES IN GERMANY

Germany has 14 national parks and biosphere reserves. Four of these are highlighted here.

The world's longest treetop walk, at 0.8 miles (1.3 km), is an attraction at the Bavarian Forest National Park.

BAVARIAN FOREST NATIONAL PARK The Bavarian Forest is a wooded low-mountain region in Bavaria. It extends along the Czech border and continues on the Czech side as the Bohemian Forest. The Bavarian Forest and the Bohemian Forest are sections of the same mountain range. A part of the Bavarian Forest belongs to the Bavarian Forest National Park, established in 1970 as the first national park in Germany.

LOWER ODER VALLEY NATIONAL PARK The Lower Oder Valley International Park is a shared German-Polish nature reserve. The German part of the core area is the Lower Oder Valley National Park. The Polish part of the core area is the Lower Odra Valley Landscape Park. The flat western shore of the Oder features several levees, which in order to control the water level and to prevent high floods are regularly opened in winter and spring. The water flows freely into extensive floodplains covered until April, when the dikes are closed again and the remaining water is drained. These plains are habitats for animals rare in the region including the black stork, the aquatic warbler, the corn crake, the European otter, and the European beaver as well as for plants such as the sub-Mediterranean pubescent oak.

MÜRITZ NATIONAL PARK The Müritz National Park is situated roughly in the middle between Berlin and Rostock, in the south of the German state of Mecklenburg-Vorpommern. It extends over large portions of the Müritz lakeland in the district of Mecklenburgische Seenplatte. Well-known animals residing in the park include the red deer, the crane, the white-tailed eagle, and the osprey. Other animals include the great bittern, the reed warbler, the redshank, the greenshank, the black stork, the crane, the teal, the garganey, and the little stint.

BERCHTESGADEN NATIONAL PARK   The Berchtesgaden National Park was established in 1978 and has gradually become one of the area's largest draws. Mass tourism is confined to a few popular spots, which gives alternative, nature-seeking tourists plenty of space to find peace and quiet in the park. Major tourist draws are Königssee Lane, the salt mine (with a sound-and-light show inaugurated in 2007), and the Eagle's Nest (Kehlsteinhaus), which occupies one of the most breathtakingly scenic spots in Germany. This former lodge had been one of the headquarters of Hitler's Nazi government; today it houses a restaurant. There is also a link through a tunnel to the Nazi bunkers in Obersalzburg, which were built in 1943.

Recreational and competitive sports have grown in importance. Although Berchtesgaden's ski slopes are not among the largest in the Alps, they can easily accommodate everyone from beginners to competitive skiers and boarders.

INTERNET LINKS

www.umweltbundesamt.de/index-e.htm

This is the official website of the German Federal Environmental Agency, which is chock-full of relevant statistics and press releases. There is also a 3D walk-through of the official agency building in Dessau.

www.makingthishome.com/2009/02/08/recycling-in-germany-practically-takes-a-phd/

A tongue-in-cheek look at recycling in Germany, which gives a clue as to why Germany is the world leader in recycling.

www.germany.travel/en/leisure-and-recreation/national-parks-nature-parks/national-parks-nature-parks.html

All about parks and reserves in Germany.

GERMANS

A girl in the traditional outfit of Gutach, Baden-Württemberg. The signature of the Black Forest costume is the *Bollenhut*. Worn during special celebrations, the hat's pom-poms can be red or black. Red for those who are single and black for those who are married.

6

APPROXIMATELY 81.2 MILLION PEOPLE live in Germany. Although Germany is the most populous nation in the EU, it has one of the lowest birth rates in the world. It is estimated that only 1.41 children are born to the average couple. This decline in the birth rate is expected to continue, as more German couples marry later in life or choose not to have children.

One in three Germans lives in a large city, and about 80 percent of the total population live in cities with a population of 100,000 or more. The majority of Germans live in the huge conurbations (continuous networks of urban communities) of the Rhine—Ruhr Valley near Cologne, the Rhine—Main area near Frankfurt, and the Swabian industrial area near Stuttgart, where jobs and recreational facilities are more plentiful.

GERMAN CHARACTERISTICS

The German nation grew from the tribes of Franks, Saxons, Bavarians, and Swabians, and these continue to be active regional groups. Although the influx of millions of displaced persons, refugees, and immigrants has influenced the German character, some stereotypes persist. Rhinelanders are thought to be easygoing, and Swabians thrifty. Those from south Germany, particularly Bavaria, are thought of as politically conservative and generally Roman Catholic; those from the north are expected to be Protestant and liberal. Berliners and people from the

Of approximately 100 million native speakers of German in the world, about 66 million to 75 million consider themselves Germans.

A family in traditional German apparel. Men and boys sport the lederhosen, while and the women and girls are in dirndls.

province of Schleswig-Holstein have a reputation for being talkative.

Germans have a love for bureaucracy, and most people obey and rarely question rules. A love of order translates into extreme neatness, and families are often very proud of their homes.

Perhaps due to their bitter experiences during the Nazi regime, Germans in general do not openly express feelings of national patriotism, preferring to pledge their loyalties to their hometown or region.

DRESS

For everyday wear, Germans choose jeans, T-shirts or sweatshirts, leather jackets, and sneakers or leather shoes. Large cities such as Berlin, Hamburg, Munich, Frankfurt, and Düsseldorf have an array of local and international boutiques with designer clothing for the fashion-conscious. Although German dress is becoming more casual on the whole, it is still acceptable to dress in full evening attire—long dresses for women, tuxedos or tails for men—when attending formal functions such as the opera or theater performances as well as high-class clubs and casinos.

Dress variations do exist among the regions, although traditional outfits are now worn mostly during festivals. Visible examples are the Baltic Sea blue jacket and trousers with a peaked cap, the Hamburg blue sailor's cap, and the Bavarian dirndl dress and apron. The famous short leather trousers, called lederhosen, are found throughout Germany.

The traditional Munich-style dress is the Bavarian *Tracht* (TRAHCT), or loden: green wool capes and jackets. Instead of lederhosen, Bavarian men might wear gray or green trousers with a waterproof woven jacket and a green felt hat topped by a pair of feathers. These costumes are worn during festive occasions, more often in rural than urban areas.

The immigrant Turkish community can easily be identified by its conservatively dressed women, who generally wear scarves rather than the full head coverings worn by Muslim women in the Middle East.

THE WITTELSBACHS

The Wittelsbach family ruled Bavaria from 1180 to 1918, first as dukes and later as monarchs. After World War I, Ludwig III formally gave up the throne, and the family gave several castles, including Neuschwanstein and Linderhof (right), and works of art to the state of Bavaria. The family still owns the Hohenschwangen Castle near Neuschwanstein, which is used as a retreat.

During the Nazi period in the 1930s and 1940s, the Wittelsbach family, led by Ludwig III's son, Prince Rupert, opposed and resisted Adolf Hitler by producing an opposition newspaper. As a result, many family members were sent to concentration camps in 1944 and 1945, spending the last days of the war in the Dachau camp until they were liberated by the American army.

Today the family still makes use of the Nymphenburg Palace in Bavaria for particular functions. Prince Rupert's son Albert, the Duke of Bavaria, played a visible role in Bavarian society until his death in 1996 at the age of 91. In 1980, when Pope John Paul II visited Bavaria, Albert was among those who greeted him.

Some people in Bavaria still call the current duke, Franz, "your royal highness." The Wittelsbach family remains popular in the region. They are closely identified with local traditions and heritage and remembered as good and kind rulers.

IMMIGRANTS AND MINORITIES

Today about 7 million people living in Germany are non-German citizens. The Turks, who number about 2 million, are the largest group of foreigners. During the period of the "economic miracle" of the 1950s and 1960s, German factories had a shortage of blue-collar labor. The German and Turkish governments signed an agreement to enable Turks to work in Germany as *Gastarbeiter* (GAST-ahr-byte-er), or guest workers. The Turks have since built their own close-knit communities in Germany. Berlin is the city with the largest Turkish population outside of Turkey.

Dachau concentration camp is where thousands of Jews were murdered by the Nazis, is the fourth-most-visited site in Germany today.

Other immigrant communities include former Yugoslavs (estimated to number about 1.5 million, including many war refugees), Poles (1.5 million), Italians (650,000), and Greeks (295,000), as well as smaller numbers of Austrians, Russians, Romanians, Spaniards, Africans, and Asians.

German reunification has brought about unemployment among the minority groups, as an abundant supply of labor from the eastern states poses competition for jobs that were usually performed by immigrants.

MINORITIES The end of the Cold War contributed to a growth in the Jewish community of Germany. Today Germany is home to a Jewish population of more than 200,000, although this number reflects non-Jewish spouses or children who also immigrated under the Quota Refugee Law, and 104,024 are officially registered with Jewish religious communities. Germany has the third largest Jewish population in Western Europe, after France (600,000) and Great Britain (300,000), and the fastest growing Jewish population in Europe in recent years.

About 60,000 Sorbians, a Slavic minority, live between the Oder and Neisse rivers. Road signs in this region are in both Sorb and German. There is also a small Frisian-speaking minority on the North Sea coast.

Today immigrant and minority workers have considerable political rights within Germany. In addition, they normally enjoy comprehensive health, education, and welfare benefits. However, some restrictions to full integration into German society still apply. Since 2005, for instance, German immigration laws allow foreigners to become German citizens only after having lived in Germany for eight years or unless they can trace their background to German ancestors. Also, all immigrants have to meet basic educational and language requirements to reduce the burden on the social security system.

CLASS DIVISIONS

The German aristocracy played a dominant role in society until 1918. They have been replaced by an industrial class of wealthy manufacturers and businesspeople, who prospered in former West Germany in the years following the end of World War II. In keeping with the traditional German values of modesty and frugality, this new class, in general, dislikes displaying its wealth in an extravagant manner.

Nevertheless, some traces of the aristocracy still remain. Romantic castles built by the long-ago aristocrats abound in Germany, and Germans whose last names begin with *von* (FOHN) can trace their ancestry to the old aristocracy. Present-day German aristocrats have retained a few privileges, such as private ownership of some small-scale castles. They generally regard their position in life as a privilege, and many are involved in social and charity work.

The upper middle class is made up of managers, professionals, and civil servants. The lower class has decreased as more and more people have attained the education, income, and lifestyle of the middle class.

Social divisions today are based largely on wealth, with differences among Germans being between the employed and the unemployed, and maybe between former East and West Germans.

INTERNET LINKS

http://germanlife.com/about-german-life/

This website displays the diversity of German culture, past and present, and in the various ways that North America has been shaped by its German element.

www.jewishvirtuallibrary.org/jsource/vjw/germany.html

A history of the Jews in Germany from the fourth century to the present, including the Nazi era.

www.spiegel.de/international/0,1518,345720,00.html

A beautiful article about how Germans today are still struggling with their Nazi past. It has links at the bottom of the page to rare photos from World War II, carefully preserved by a photographer who buried his negatives until 1970—another amazing story to read.

In Germany it is a criminal act to deny the Holocaust or that 6 million Jews were murdered in the Holocaust. Violations can be punished with up to five years in prison. At the same time, it is thought there are almost 10,000 neo-Nazis in Germany, and a national database would include information held by all federal and state authorities.

Locals resting and shopping at the main train station in Leipzig, Saxony.

M

OST GERMANS SPEND THEIR work and leisure time in the same ways as people in other Western countries. Families are generally small and nuclear, consisting of only father, mother, and one or two children, particularly in urban areas.

Often both parents work in order to keep up with the high cost of living. Young people dress casually in jeans and T-shirts. American culture is very influential in Germany and American sitcoms, sports events, and popular music are closely followed by the youth.

7

Germany was ranked fourth in the world in a 2011 Mercer Quality of Living Survey, behind Austria, Switzerland, and New Zealand.

Young boys being coached at a mini-league football game.

Gabled houses and stores line the historic Marketplace in Bremen.

Within Germany, there remain great variations in lifestyle—between the urban and the rural, the different localities, the employed and the unemployed, the former East and West Germans.

HOUSING

Many Germans dream of owning a house with a garden. About 42 percent of Germans living in the western states own their homes, which generally come with all modern conveniences. Seventy percent of housing in the western states has been built since 1945. Rent and mortgage payments make up a high proportion of a family's monthly expenses.

Architectural styles vary throughout Germany, depending on local building materials and the climate. In the Alpine area, chalet-style houses are built on south-facing slopes. In North Rhine-Westphalia, half-timbered houses have slates covering their western walls for protection against the biting wind. Some city residential areas offer restored 19th-century blocks of buildings for sale or rental. High-rise blocks with basic facilities are available for lower-income families in some suburban areas.

FAMILY LIFE

In urban areas both spouses must work to be able to afford the contemporary German's ideal lifestyle: home ownership and overseas vacations. The size of the German family is decreasing. On average, a family has just one or two children. In the rural areas of southern Germany, families with several generations living under the same roof can be found, but this is rare in urban areas. The population mainly consists of families with unmarried children or of married couples who are childless or no longer have children living at home. Germany's percentage of single-person households has been rising slowly but steadily for years, reaching 39.5 percent in 2009. Of Germany's household heads, 11.6 percent are 30 or under. Of Germany's 8.4 million families with children, 1.6 million, or one in five families, are headed by a single parent. Ten years ago, the figure was just 14 percent.

People are relatively free to marry whom they choose, and marriage is no longer the only option. Forty percent of couples between the ages of 18 and 35 live together without being legally married. Children of unmarried parents have the same legal rights as children of traditional marriages.

Fathers in Germany coming together to discuss their babies. In the modern German society, both fathers and mothers are equally involved in raising the family.

CHILDHOOD RITUALS

Babies are christened or baptized soon after their birth, regardless of whether they come from a Protestant or Catholic family. For Catholics, the child's first communion at the age of seven years is an important event. For Protestants, confirmation at around 14 years of age is a major occasion. In present-day secular society, however, the first day at school is replacing religious rituals as the most important occasion in a child's life.

YOUTH

Friends and family cheering on a newly wedded couple in Berlin.

Just 13.3 percent of the population is under 14 years of age. To encourage couples to have children, tax breaks are given for each child. In addition, a child's education is free from elementary school to university. Many laws protect the rights of children, and child pornography is strictly prohibited. As in many other modern westernized societies, despite their material wealth, drug addiction is a problem for some young people in urban areas.

WEDDINGS

During the engagement period, German couples wear a gold ring on the fourth finger of the left hand. In order to be legally married couples must go through a civil ceremony in a registry office (often in the town hall). Family and friends gather outside the town hall to throw rice and flowers at the newlyweds as they emerge from the town hall. Only the civil marriage is considered legal in Germany.

The church wedding, generally on the weekend after the civil ceremony, is optional but still popular with couples who belong to a church and pay church taxes. During the religious ceremony, small page boys and flower girls enter

A well-tended cemetery in Baden-Württemberg.

the church followed by the bride and the groom. The gold engagement rings are moved from the left to the right hand of both the bride and the groom during the service. After the ceremony, there is usually a reception for family and friends, with food and drinks, speeches, and dancing. The 25th and 50th wedding anniversaries are family celebrations.

DEATHS

Deaths are announced in the newspapers. Relatives send black-rimmed notifications of the funeral arrangements to friends and acquaintances.

Funerals are a time of family reunion where support is given to the deceased's family. German families rarely hold full wakes these days, as wakes are mostly confined to small, conservative Catholic towns. Calla lilies, tall white flowers, are the traditional flowers for funeral services.

It is customary for the surviving partner to wear both wedding rings as a sign of widowhood. Graves are tended regularly, and full mourning dress (black clothes) can be worn.

WOMEN

According to the Basic Law, women enjoy the same legal rights as men. In actual employment, however, inequalities do exist. Within marriage, laws protect women's property rights. Husband and wife can take either the woman's or the man's last name, keep their own names, or choose both names—a *Doppelname* (DOH-pull-NAH-meh)—without adding a hyphen.

In the case of divorce, the wealthier partner continues to support the other regardless of who is responsible for the breakup of the marriage.

Women employees are more likely to become unemployed during a recession, and fewer are promoted into top posts. Male employees still receive higher wages than their female counterparts. It is a conundrum in Germany that while women are not well represented at all in the higher echelons of business, they do surprisingly well in politics. Germany ranks 18th in the world for female participation in the national parliament with just over 32 percent of representatives in the Bundestag being women.

SHOPPING

Large supermarkets and shopping centers are located in the center of most German cities. Most stores close at 6:30 P.M. on weekdays and 2:00 P.M. on Saturdays. Some stay open until 8:00 P.M. on weekdays and 4:00 P.M. on Saturdays. The first Saturday of every month is known as *langer Samstag* (LAHNG-ur SAHMS-tahg), or "long Saturday," when stores close at 6:00 P.M. All stores used to be closed on Sundays, following the 1956 Shop Closure Law.

EDUCATION

Education is compulsory for children from the ages of 6 to 18 years. The school year runs from the end of August to June or July, with a half-year assessment report in February. There is a six-week summer vacation and two weeks' vacation during Christmas and Easter. The length and time of the vacations differ from state to state. The school day lasts from 8:00 A.M. to 1:00 P.M., Monday through Friday, and from 8:00 A.M. to noon on Saturday. School hours are devoted almost completely to academic subjects, with few nonacademic activities. Children return home for lunch after school and spend the afternoon doing their homework.

German children begin elementary school, or, *Grundschule* (GROONT-shoo-leh), at the age of six. Elementary school lasts four or five years, depending on the state. At around the age of 10, children must choose among three types of schools: *Hauptschule* (HOWPT-shoo-leh), *Realschule* (RAY-ahl-shoo-leh), and *Gymnasium* (ghim-NAH-zee-um).

About one-half of the children progress to *Hauptschule*, where they continue to receive full-time general education until the age of 15 or 16. After *Hauptschule*, pupils proceed to a part-time vocational school. About one-third of the students proceed to *Realschule*, where they receive a comprehensive general education. A *Realschule* certificate qualifies students to proceed to a technical school. Less than one-fourth of children proceed to *Gymnasium*, which prepares students to take the *Abitur* (AH-bee-toor) exam after nine years of study, a requirement to enter university.

TYPES OF SCHOOL AND FURTHER EDUCATION Most German children attend state schools; about 10 percent attend private schools—usually run by churches—and 13 percent attend the free Waldorf schools, where equal emphasis is placed on academic and artistic subjects. Each state runs its own education system and appoints teachers. However, teachers are subject to the authority of the Federal Ministry of Education.

Students at a high-school class in the town of Hannoversch Münden, situated in the Weser Valley. Some of the Weser Renaissance buildings in this town are more than 600 years old.

One unique feature of the German education system is a forest kindergarten: a type of preschool education for children between the ages of three and six that is held almost exclusively outdoors. Whatever the weather, children are encouraged to play, explore, and learn in a forest or natural environment.

Founded in 1810, the prestigious Humboldt University of Berlin has produced numerous famous scholars and Nobel Prize winners.

German universities have a long tradition of academic excellence. However, the large number of applicants has resulted in overcrowded facilities. Student places are usually awarded on the basis of the applicant's *Abitur* exam. Courses of study in new technological fields have been introduced to keep pace with current industrial trends. University courses culminate in either a *Magister* (MAH-ghee-steh) or a *Diplom* (DIH-plohm) examination or a state examination.

University education is free of charge or costs only a nominal fee at present, but the economic downturn has sparked a debate on whether students should be made to pay their own tuition.

HEALTH CARE

Health care in Germany is well funded and equipped, providing health insurance for all employees, the self-employed, and their dependents, regardless of their nationality. The lower-income groups and the unemployed are provided for by state and federal projects. Still, occasional abuses to the system are reported.

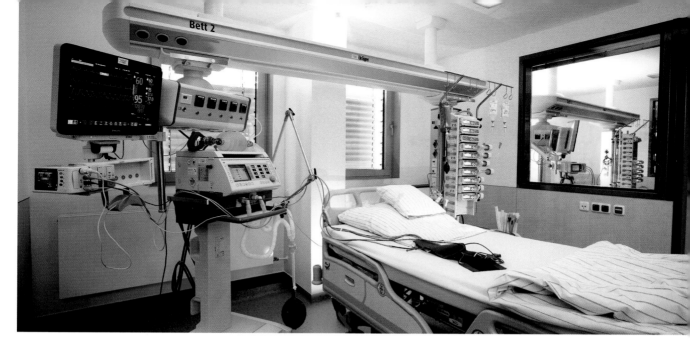

An intensive care unit with multiple life-support systems at a hospital in Germany.

There were 325,945 doctors in Germany at the end of 2009. They work in private practice or in one of the general hospitals. Germans are offered three mandatory health benefits, which are cofinanced by employer and employee: health insurance, accident insurance, and long-term-care insurance. Although different in conditions, these health schemes also extend to the unemployed, or recipients of social benefit allowances in the country.

INTERNET LINKS

www.telegraph.co.uk/education/3357232/Waldkindergarten-the-forest-nurseries-where-children-learn-in-Natures-classroom.html

A charming article on forest kindergartens.

www.journey-to-germany.com/education.html

A comprehensive explanation of education in Germany.

www.npr.org/series/91971170/germany-health-care-for-all

A website on health care in Germany with the latest articles and updated information.

The average length of a hospital stay in Germany has decreased in recent years from 14 days to 9 days, still considerably longer than the average stay of 5-6 days in the United States.

RELIGION

The towering and beautiful Cologne Cathedral is a Roman Catholic church in Cologne. The construction of this Gothic masterpiece began in 1248 and was only completed in 1880.

8

GERMANY IS A SECULAR STATE, with freedom of religion guaranteed by the Basic Law. All registered members of large Christian denominations—Roman Catholic, Calvinist, Lutheran—and Jewish synagogues must pay a church tax.

More than 50 million people in Germany (68 percent of the population) belong to a Christian church—27.7 million are Protestant, and 25.4 million are Roman Catholic. Although only a small percentage of German Christians attend church on Sundays, Sunday is still regarded as a day of rest in Germany. Most stores are closed, and there are strict rules about performing any type of work on Sundays.

Article 4 of the German constitution guarantees freedom of religion: Each person has the right to freely choose and practice his or her religion. This religious freedom also includes the right to change from one faith to another.

The lavish interiors of the Asamkirche, or Asam Church, in Munich. Built from 1733 to 1746, this was once a private church.

Service held at a Protestant church in Germany.

The former East Germany had no religious instruction in school, and socialist rites replaced religious ceremonies at birth, marriage, and death.

The *Jugendweihe* (YOO-gund-vye-eh) was established by the East German government in the 1950s as a secular coming-of-age ritual meant to replace the rite of confirmation in Christian churches. Sociologists have observed that many eastern Germans, 10 years after reunification, are experiencing *Ostalgie* (OHST-ahl-ghee), defined as "eastern nostalgia," and developing a distinct eastern identity rooted in the experience of life in the former Deutsche Demokratische Republik. As a result, the *Jugendweihe*, which briefly fell out of fashion after unification, has regained popularity among eastern teenagers and their parents.

CHURCH IN SOCIETY

Many leading members of the Protestant and Catholic churches stood up against Adolf Hitler during World War II, and as a result, the churches see themselves as protectors of freedom and democracy. This proved to be true again in 1989 when church members played a big part in the downfall of communist East Germany and the reemergence of democracy in that part of the country.

The German church, thanks to a compulsory church tax, is the wealthiest Catholic church in Europe.

Both Protestant and Catholic churches run a variety of social services—schools, kindergartens, nursing homes, programs for the disabled, hospitals, and other organizations—that fill a social need and are offered to people of all religious backgrounds.

The country is broadly divided between a mainly Protestant north and a Catholic south. However, the large influx of refugees from Eastern Europe in 1945, as well as of East Germans during the 1940s and 1950s, has served to blur these lines and give more communities a mixed-Christian population.

CATHOLICISM

The predominantly Catholic areas of Germany have traditionally been Rhineland-Palatinate, Saarland, and Bavaria, with an equal number of Catholics and Protestants in Baden-Württemberg and North Rhine-Westphalia. The Catholic Church in Germany consists of five church provinces with seven archbishoprics and 22 bishoprics. The colorful festivals of Corpus Christi and Ascension Day are celebrated in Catholic areas.

Cardinals and acolytes attending a Mass at Saint Mary's Cathedral in Freising.

PROTESTANTISM

Protestants in Germany for the most part belong to one of three denominations: Lutheran, Reformed (Calvinist or Zwinglian), or United (a combination of Reformed and Lutheran). Protestantism is practiced predominantly in the north. Churches are grouped into an alliance of 24 mostly independent churches known as the Evangelische Kirche in Deutschland, or EKD, at the top of which is a synod for legislative matters and a council for executive matters. Most Lutheran churches are also grouped into the United Evangelical Lutheran Church of Germany, or the VELKD.

There are also "free" churches, which are affiliated with smaller Protestant denominations such as Baptists and Pentecostals. The Methodists and the Evangelical community have joined to become the Evangelical Methodist Church. There are small numbers of Quakers, Mennonites, and members of the Salvation Army, well known for their social and educational work.

OTHER BELIEFS

JUDAISM The Jewish population in Germany before 1933 was about 600,000, but due to the horrors of the Holocaust that number was reduced to 2,000 at the end of World War II. Today about 200,000 Jews live in Germany, most

At least one Jewish cemetery is desecrated each week in Germany.

It was in Germany that Christianity first split into Roman Catholicism and Protestantism. In 1517 Martin Luther, an Augustinian monk, criticized the Catholic Church for selling "indulgences" as a means of fund-raising. An indulgence was the temporary forgiveness of sins before final absolution was granted after confession. The money raised from the selling of indulgences funded the building of such beautiful and imposing churches as Saint Peter's Church in Rome. Corruption was common among church leaders of the time. Luther argued for equality between layperson and priest, disputed the pope's authority and the role of the clergy, and asserted the individual's right to read the Scriptures for himself or herself, translating the Bible from Greek to German to help people do so.

Luther's moral protest was adopted for political ends by a number of German princes. His protest against the Church's abuse of authority indirectly triggered the Peasants' War in 1524, which was forcibly put down by the princes. Religious wars in the 16th and 17th centuries killed many Germans and reduced the country to a series of up to 350 principalities in the 18th century.

of them having immigrated from areas of the former Soviet Union. There are Jewish congregations throughout Germany, with the largest in Berlin and in Frankfurt, Germany's banking center, which was largely started by Jews. Acts of atonement have been performed by former German leaders at Israel's monuments to World War II, and reparations were agreed upon and paid to Israel during the 1970s. The reluctance of large numbers of Jews to return to Germany has deprived the country of much creative talent. Recently, anti-Semitism has resurfaced in some areas of the country, particularly in the eastern states.

ISLAM The large Turkish minority, mainly concentrated in Berlin, makes up the bulk of Germany's Muslims. It is estimated that about 3.9 million Muslims from 41 nations live in Germany. Islam is the largest minority religion in Germany. Rights of worship, education, and religious schooling are all guaranteed under German law. German employers often set aside rooms to allow Muslim employees to carry out their daily prayers. The Muslim festival of Ramadan and observances and arrangements for the pilgrimage to Mecca are all carried out with the help of religious leaders and government bodies. The government works with Turkey to bring religious teachers to Germany to preach to its Turkish minority. Liberal rather than fundamentalist preachers are preferred, so that the Turks will have fewer problems integrating into German society.

ATHEISM Less than a third of the German population are either atheist or simply uninterested in religion. This is particularly common in urban centers, especially Berlin, and in the former East Germany, where atheism was encouraged and taught, even though religious freedom was allowed.

Although Germany is a secular state, Christianity still has a great effect on culture, personal attitudes, social structure, and even politics. One of the ruling political parties, the Christian Democratic Union, is strongly supported by Catholics and Protestants.

INTERNET LINKS

www.pbs.org/empires/martinluther/
A fascinating website on Martin Luther.

www.deutschland.de/en/religion/religious-persuasions.html
A comprehensive website on religion in Germany today with links to a website for each faith.

http://nobeliefs.com/nazis.htm
A collection of Nazi-era photos showing religious practice under Hitler.

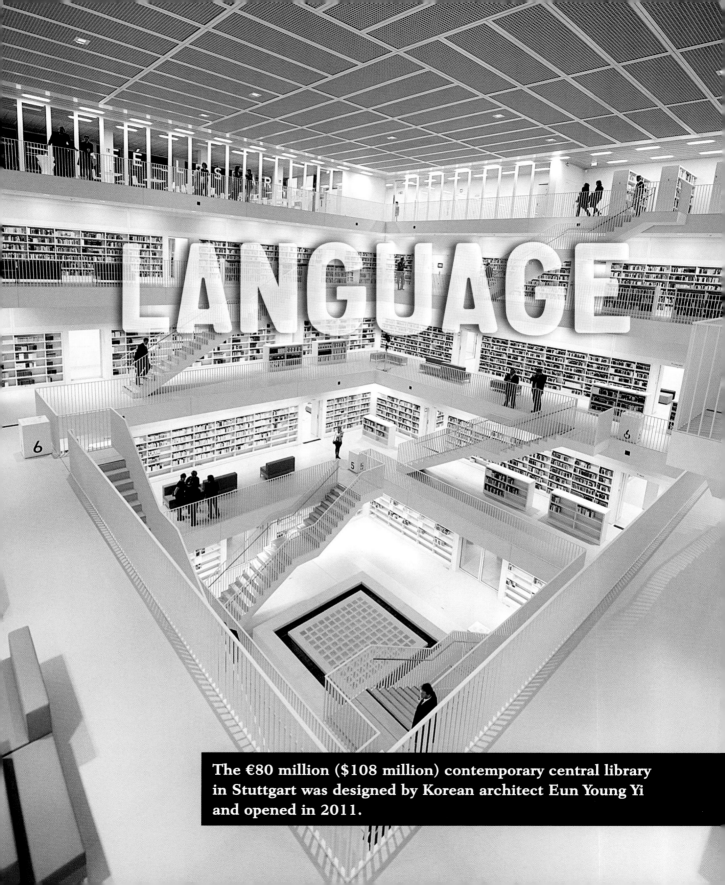

The €80 million ($108 million) contemporary central library in Stuttgart was designed by Korean architect Eun Young Yi and opened in 2011.

GERMAN IS SPOKEN throughout Germany and in parts of neighboring Luxembourg, Switzerland, the Netherlands, Italy, and Austria. This common language was a uniting force among the people long before Germany became a nation, and it remains a common bond among the states and regions today.

The language is changing, with increasing additions from other Western languages, particularly American and British English.

Various automobile magazines on sale at a store in Germany.

9

With an estimated 90 million to 98 million native speakers, German is one of the world's major languages and is the most widely spoken first language in the European Union.

The Latin Vulgate Gutenberg Bible, printed in 1454 by Johannes Gutenberg, was one of Germany's first printed books.

Together with German, Frisian is spoken along the North Sea coast; Danish just along the frontier with Denmark in Schleswig-Holstein; and Slavonic Sorbian in parts of Lusatia, Berlin, and east of the Elbe River. Many Germans speak English fluently, and many former East Germans can converse in Russian.

THE GERMAN LANGUAGE

As the English language has Germanic roots, many German words are similar to English words, in both meaning and pronunciation: *gut* (good), *buch* (book), *fein* (fine), *haus* (house), *preis* (price). Perhaps the most peculiar characteristic about German is the length of some words. These are generally compound words, which explain a combined meaning that could easily take a whole phrase in English to translate. Several German words have crept into the English language—for example, *kindergarten*, *wanderlust*, *rucksack*, *hinterland*, and *leitmotif*.

German grammar can seem overwhelmingly complicated to English speakers. The language uses three genders (neuter, male, and female) and four cases (nominative, dative, accusative, and genitive). Each noun starts with a capital letter, and any qualifying adjectives agree in gender and case with the noun. German word order is quite unlike that of English, with the verb falling at the end of the sentence rather than following immediately after the subject.

SCRIPT

If you look at written German, you may come across a curious sign, ß, nowadays written as ss, which is pronounced "tz." Another is a letter that resembles an f, but is in fact the way an s is written at the beginning of a word. Both characters are no longer commonly used in today's newspapers. Several German newspapers use versions of the old German script for their title letterings. Original works by Johann Wolfgang von Goethe and Friedrich Schiller written in this old style are almost unrecognizable today.

PRONUNCIATION

Pronunciation is generally straightforward, with the stress on the root of a word, often the first syllable. Consonants are broadly pronounced as in English, though some combinations differ. These are listed below.

Letter(s)	Example	Pronunciation
ch	acht	guttural ch as in Scottish "loch"
chs	sechs	ks as in "wakes"
d	und	t as in "wait" at the end of a word, otherwise as in English
pf	pferd	pf—the "p" is pronounced subtly
qu	qualität	kv—no equivalent in English
s	sie	z as in "zoo" at the beginning of a word
v	vögel	f as in "full" at the beginning of a word, otherwise as in English
w	wir	v as in "vex"

One reason foreigners find German difficult to understand is that a number of words are compounds of smaller words. Multiple nouns can be joined, such as Rathaus, which is a compound of rat (parliament) and haus (house). So the compound Rathaus means "the building where the parliament meets."

Vowels and vowel combinations are pronounced differently than in English, although they generally follow the rules below.

Letter(s)	Example	Pronunciation
a	land	short a as in "hat"
a	name	soft a as in "father"
ä	länder	e sound as in "lender"
ai	kaiser	long i as in "height"
au	haus	ow as in "house"
äu	häuser	oy as in "soil"
e	sechs	short e as in "set"
e	dritte	unstressed, like "e" in "open"
ee	nordsee	ay as in "say"
ei	weiss	long i as in "white"
eu	euch	oy as in "soil"
i	Ich	short i as in "in"
ie	sie	ee sound as in "tea"
o	wo	long o as in "woe"
o	doppel	short o as in "on"
ö	löffel	er as in "berth"
u	buch	oo as in "boot"
ü	bücher	fine u, like "unique" without the y sound

As the table shows, vowels with umlauts (two dots over letters) are pronounced differently from those without. When publishers are unable to set umlauts, an extra e is added to indicate altered pronunciation (and often meaning). For instance, bücher can be written as buecher.

HIGH AND LOW GERMAN

High German is German that is traditionally spoken in central Germany and is now accepted and taught as the standard language. Low German is the language spoken on the low, flat northern plain and is regarded as a dialect, just like Bavarian in the south of Germany.

The main difference between the two languages was caused by the German Sound Shift, which occurred between the fifth and eighth centuries, whereby in High German the consonant *p* became *f* or *pf*, *t* became *ss* or *z*, and *k* became *ch*. Thus:

Low German	slapen	appel	water	tid
High German	schlafen	apfel	wasser	zeit
English	sleep	apple	water	time

FORMS OF ADDRESS

In Germany there are different ways of addressing people, depending on how well you know them, their social or professional status, whether they are older or younger than you, and so on. The most polite word for *you*, in both the singular and plural form, is *sie* (zee), which Germans use in direct address until they become familiar with the person they are speaking with. It is similar in English to calling people *Mr.* or *Mrs.* until they invite you to call them by their first name.

However, it would not be considered unusual or rude to continue addressing business associates in a long-term working relationship using the formal *sie*. First names are rarely heard in offices. *Herr* (HAIR) or *Frau* (FROW) so-and-so remains the usual form of address at work, particularly among older people. A gulf separates one's office and private lives.

Close friends, siblings, and young people in general use the informal *du* (DOO) to address one another. Parents use *du* when talking to their children. University students use *du* regardless of age differences but not before asking, "Can we call each other *du*?"

A lawyer, a doctor, or a professor should be addressed with a professional title—for example, *Frau Doktor* or *Herr Professor*. Old aristocratic families can be recognized by *von* in the surname, as in *Marion von Döhnhoff*, former publisher of the weekly *Die Zeit*.

Common German greetings are straightforward, depending on the time of day. Rather than "hello," Germans say "*guten morgen*" (GOO-ten MORR-gen), or "good morning"; "*guten tag*" (GOO-ten TAHG), or "good day"; and "*guten abend*" (GOO-ten AH-bent), or "good evening." "goodbye" is "*auf wiedersehen*" (OWF VEE-der-zay-en), or "Until we meet again." Between friends and family, a less formal goodbye is "*tschüss*" (CHHUSS), or "see you."

THE MEDIA

Germany's television market is the largest in Europe, with some 34 million TV households. Around 90 percent of German households have cable or satellite TV, and viewers enjoy a comprehensive mix of free-to-view public and commercial channels. This has acted as a brake on the development of pay-TV. While the press and broadcasters are free and independent, the display of swastikas and statements endorsing Nazism are illegal.

There are several national newspapers, but the press market is strongest at a regional level, with more than 300 titles. Bild *tabloid is the best-selling daily. By March 2011, nearly 80 percent of Germans—65.1 million people—were online, InternetWorldStats reported. The leading social network is Facebook, with more than 20 million users. Its rivals include Wer-kennt-wen and MeinVZ.*

BODY LANGUAGE AND ETIQUETTE

Social interaction is often quite formal in Germany. People shake hands when introduced or when greeting people they already know, and they are protective of their personal space and privacy. At mealtimes it is impolite to start eating before your host has wished you "*guten appetit*" (GOOT-en ahp-eh-TEET).

Unlike people from Mediterranean cultures, Germans tend to use little facial expression when speaking to one another.

INTERNET LINKS

www.ejc.net/media_landscape/article/germany/

A comprehensive overview of the German media scene.

http://german.about.com/

A beginner's guide to the German language.

www.bbc.co.uk/languages/german/

The British Broadcasting Corporation's guide to the German language, this site has both beginner and intermediate levels.

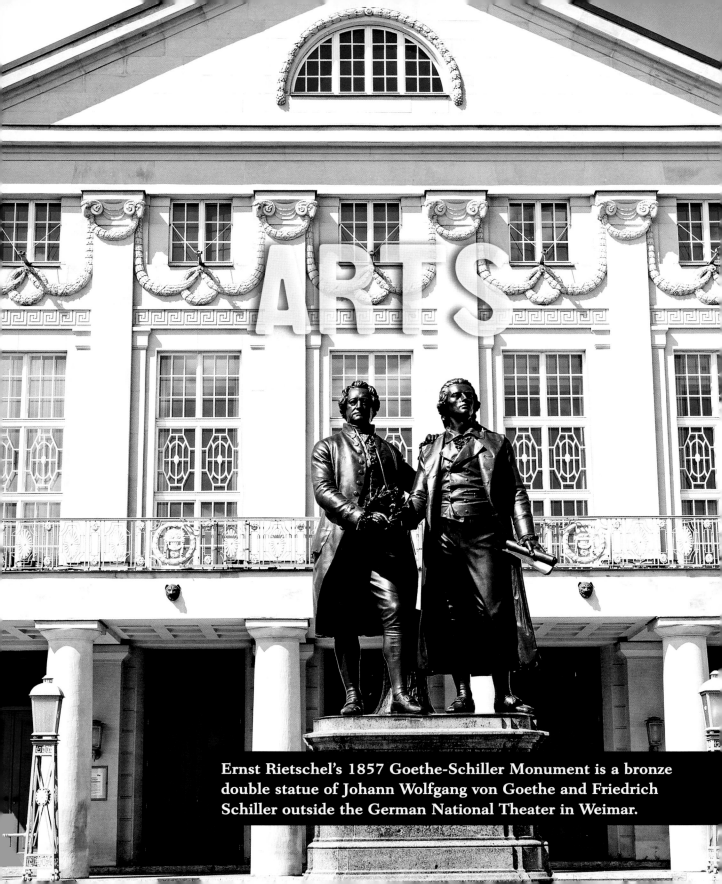

Ernst Rietschel's 1857 Goethe-Schiller Monument is a bronze double statue of Johann Wolfgang von Goethe and Friedrich Schiller outside the German National Theater in Weimar.

10

THROUGHOUT THE CENTURIES, Germany has been the cradle of European music, literature, theater, and fine arts. From Beethoven and Bach to Goethe, Heine, and Schiller, Germany has produced some of the finest composers and writers in the history of the civilized world. A strong cultural tradition remains in present-day Germany, and local musical and theatrical performances are always well patronized.

MUSIC

Germans are passionately fond of music, poetry, and drama. Almost every town in Germany has a small theater or opera house, its own amateur troupe, an orchestra or a small musical group, and maybe a choral society. Music and singing play a big part in social activities and public celebrations.

Germany has more than 130 professional orchestras, including famous ones such as the Berlin Philharmonic Orchestra, the Munich Philharmonic Orchestra, and the Bamberg Symphonic Orchestra. There are more than 200 government-subsidized opera houses and concert halls, of which Hamburg's (founded in 1678) is the oldest, as well as 1,000 theaters and 3,000 museums.

For several centuries, Germany has enjoyed a tradition of governmental support of the arts. Before the founding of the German Empire in 1871, the many small kingdoms, principalities, duchies, bishoprics, and free cities that preceded it established theaters, museums, and libraries. Their leaders acted as patrons for poets, writers, painters, and performers. The institutions they founded and their legacy of generosity towards the arts continues today.

The Semperoper is the state opera house in the historic center of Dresden. Built by architect Gottfried Semper in 1841, the opera house has a long history of premieres, including major works by Richard Wagner and Richard Strauss.

Classical recordings under famous conductors such as Herbert von Karajan have sold in the millions worldwide. Radio orchestras reach out to those who are unable to attend live performances. Artistic festivals occur frequently, celebrating famous local composers, playwrights, or performers.

Music education is strongly supported by the government. Conservatories, music colleges, and youth councils encourage young people to develop their talents in performing, as well as in listening to, all types of music. Local choral groups and quartets are active throughout the country.

GREAT MUSICIANS

Music, like language, knows no boundaries, and composers based in Austria, such as Wolfgang Amadeus Mozart, Christoph Gluck, and Franz Haydn, are often regarded as part of German musical culture.

Johann Sebastian Bach (1685—1750) was born in Eisenach, Thuringia, and worked as a choir director in Leipzig for much of his life. He composed organ pieces and orchestral works in the Baroque style. His works include the Brandenburg Concertos and church music like the St. Matthew Passion.

George Frideric Handel (1685—1759) traveled widely throughout Italy and England. He composed operas, the famous oratorio *The Messiah*, and the orchestral suites *The Water Music* and *Music for the Royal Fireworks*.

Ludwig van Beethoven (1770—1827) was born in Bonn and studied under Haydn and Mozart in Vienna. A prolific composer, his works include 32 piano sonatas, five piano concertos, nine symphonies, 17 string quartets, one opera

In 1864, after years of financial difficulties and strong controversy surrounding his works, German writer and composer Richard Wagner won the support of the young king of Bavaria, Ludwig II, a fervent admirer of his works. The king set up Wagner and his family in a villa in the small Bavarian town of Bayreuth. Wagner named the villa Wahnfried, which means "peace from illusion." Today it houses a museum dedicated to Wagner's life and works.

Thanks to the full support and sponsorship of the king, Wagner was able to fulfill his lifelong dream of building an opera house dedicated to German music and composers. In 1876 the Festspielhaus was completed, and it opened with Wagner's Ring Cycle *operas, which consist of* Rhinegold, The Valkyrie, Siegfried, *and* The Twilight of the Gods. *In 1882 Wagner's last work, the opera* Parsifal, *premiered at the Festspielhaus.*

Since then, the Festspielhaus has been holding the Richard Wagner Festival every summer, closing only during the two World Wars. Today the festival is organized by Wagner's great-granddaughters, Katharina Wagner and Eva Wagner-Pasquier, who took over the direction of the Bayreuth Festspielhaus from their father, Wolfgang Wagner, when he resigned at age 89. Wolfgang Wagner had taken over the organization of the festival from his mother in 1951. Although Wagner had originally envisioned the theater as a general showcase for German music, only his works are performed during the festival today.

(*Fidelio*), and numerous overtures. He became deaf at the age of 30 and was thus unable to hear many of his works performed.

Felix Mendelssohn (1809—47), a successor of Beethoven, traveled widely in Britain and Italy. He composed the overture *Fingal's Cave* and the Fourth "Italian" Symphony. Robert Schumann (1810—56) composed numerous piano pieces and chamber music, as well as four symphonies. Richard Wagner (1813—83) intensified the emotional content of the Romantic style in his numerous operas. Johannes Brahms (1833—97) developed a classic Romantic style in his symphonies, piano concertos, and other works.

Richard Strauss (1864—1949) wrote operas that include *Der Rosenkavalier* and many instrumental pieces. Paul Hindemith (1895—1963) composed post-Romantic instrumental music. Carl Orff (1895—1982) wrote operas and dramatic works, such as *Carmina Burana*, based on a 13th-century collection of Bavarian songs. Two other influential German composers are Hans Werner Henze (b. 1926) and Karlheinz Stockhausen (b. 1928).

The German Jazz Festival in Berlin.

BEETHOVEN'S SYMPHONIES A radical departure from previous musical styles, these works celebrated emotion and developed themes at length.

The Third Symphony was at first dedicated to Napoleon Bonaparte but was altered when the leader's violent and cruel nature became apparent to Beethoven. It was renamed *Sinfonia Eroica*, or "Heroic Symphony."

The Fifth Symphony, or Victory Symphony, has one of the most famous openings in all of music: three short notes followed by a long one.

The Sixth Symphony, or Pastoral Symphony, has a rural theme and opens with a springlike awakening in which birdsongs can be heard.

The Ninth "Choral" Symphony contains the rousing setting of Schiller's "Ode to Joy" in its final choral movement. After 1990, this orchestral music was adopted as the European anthem.

JAZZ

In the 1960s German musicians began experimenting with free jazz, a form of jazz that began in the United States in the late 1950s. German free jazz is characterized by the wild combination of different types of sounds, from contemporary classical music to strange experimental tones. Several German jazz musicians, such as pianist Alexander von Schlippenbach, trombonist Albert Mangelsdorff, trumpeter Manfred Schoof, and saxophone player Gunter Hampel, have produced innovative free-jazz pieces. The annual jazz festival in Berlin offers a showcase for jazz performers.

POP AND ROCK

German pop and rock bands such as the Scorpions, H-Bloxx, Modern Talking, and U96 have had international success. Germany's Gregorian chants of the eighth and ninth centuries have made a surprising appearance in the pop charts, adapted by the group Enigma.

MOVIES

In the 1920s Fritz Lang was one of the leading names in German cinema, along with Ernst Lubitsch, F. W. Murnau, and G. W. Pabst.

During the Hitler years, creative activity was repressed, and filmmaking was used mostly for propaganda purposes. Immediately after the war, with more urgent matters to attend to, Germany disregarded the role of movies. But in the 1960s the New German Cinema movement, echoing in some ways France's New Wave, took place. Creative individuals such as Alexander Kluge, Volker Schlöndorff, Rainer Werner Fassbinder, and then Werner Herzog, Wim Wenders, and Margarethe von Trotta came into the forefront of the industry.

Successful German filmmakers of this modern era include Wolfgang Petersen, who has established himself in Hollywood with films such as *Troy* (2004) and *Poseidon* (2006); Tom Tykwer, who directed *Run Lola Run* (1998); Patrick Süskind's *Perfume: The Story of a Murderer* (2006) and *The International* (2009); and Robert Schwentke, who made a film adaptation of Audrey Niffenegger's popular novel—*The Time Traveler's Wife* (2009). Another well-known personality is German producer Bernd Eichinger, who produced numerous *Resident Evil* films and *Fantastic Four: Rise of the Silver Surfer* (2007).

ZDF (Zweites Deutsches Fernsehen), the German Television Council, is Germany's national public television broadcaster. It is an independent non-profit corporation controlled by the cultural ministries of the federal states.

THEATER

In the 17th and 18th centuries, the individual German kingdoms and principalities set up their own state theaters and encouraged and competed for the best playwrights and actors. Today there are more than 350 theaters in Germany, 160 of them publicly owned. They receive generous government subsidies so that performances remain affordable for the average member of the public.

German drama started in earnest with the works of Gotthold Ephraim Lessing (1729—81), Johann Wolfgang von Goethe (1749—1832), and Friedrich Schiller (1759—1805). Goethe, a voice of the Romantic movement, wrote about

Fritz Lang's movie, *The Last Will of Dr. Mabuse*, showed a madman speaking Nazi philosophy. This scene attracted the attention of Nazi propaganda chief Joseph Goebbels, who asked Lang to supervise German movies. Lang refused to be associated with the Nazis and left the country that very day, moving to the United States.

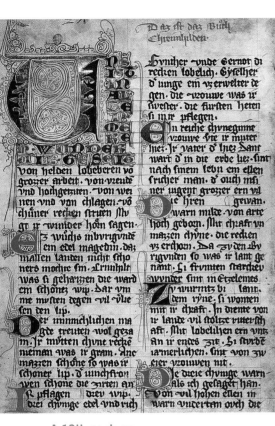

the emotional, apolitical individual, with terror lurking just beneath the surface of a peaceful scene. Schiller felt that the theater should have the moral role of instructing the audience, a viewpoint shared by Germans today. In addition to works by these three authors, Shakespearean plays are also performed regularly in German theaters.

Later German dramatists include Bertolt Brecht (1898—1956) and Peter Weiss (1916—82), whose play *Marat/Sade* was a revolutionary theatrical experiment. Günter Grass's highly political play *The Plebeians Rehearse the Uprising* is based on the 1953 uprising in East Germany. Heiner Müller's plays analyze Germany's past and present, while Harald Mueller's *Totenfloss* shows a vision of the world after a nuclear disaster. Modern-day women dramatists in Germany include Gerlinde Reinshagen and Friederike Roth.

Open-air theaters spring up throughout Germany during the summer. The Mulheim Theater Days Festival stages new plays each year.

LITERATURE

In German literature, the *Nibelungenlied*, an epic poem written around A.D. 1200, has been considered an early literary milestone. It consists of two parts—the tragic love story of Siegfried and the annihilation of the Burgundians by the Huns.

Three centuries later, Martin Luther, the founder of Protestantism, translated the Bible into German at the same time that the printing press was developed by Johannes Gutenberg. These two events greatly contributed to the widening use of written German.

During the 19th century, Theodor Fontane (1819—98), a popular realist fiction writer, and poet Rainer Maria Rilke (1875—1926) emerged as important literary figures. After the German Empire was founded in 1871, many writers focused on German patriotism and nationalism. Influential philosopher Friedrich Nietzsche, however, criticized these values.

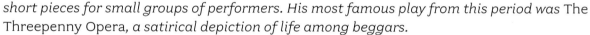
Bertolt Brecht (1898—1956) was a prolific playwright who developed a unique style of "epic theater." His plays imitated the deeds of humanity through an "alienation device," presenting familiar events and actions in a strange way but generally avoiding either approval or condemnation of these actions. It was left to the audience to judge the right or wrong of the situations presented, a judgment that Brecht hoped audiences would continue to act on when they left the theater.

He founded a school literary magazine at 15, writing short pieces and his first play in his late teens. His early ideas and beliefs were destroyed by World War I, and his experience of war comes through in Baal *and* Drums in the Night. *Brecht wrote numerous plays during the 1920s, including* In the Jungle of Cities *and* The Rise and Fall of the City of Mahagonny, *as well as a series of short pieces for small groups of performers. His most famous play from this period was* The Threepenny Opera, *a satirical depiction of life among beggars.*

Two plays written in 1931, when he had become a Marxist, The Mother *and* Saint Joan of the Stockyards, *were hardly performed at the time because of their highly critical views on the failing Weimar Republic.* Saint Joan *depicted a chilling example of how capitalism could exploit people.*

Brecht left Germany in February 1933—the day after a fire destroyed the German parliament and showed the true nature of the Nazi regime—traveling to Denmark, Sweden, Finland, the Soviet Union, and finally the United States. In exile, he developed the theory that the beginning of fascism lies in the economic crisis of capitalism. He produced antifascist plays, such as Round Heads and Pointed Heads *(which saw racism as a diversion from the real contest between exploiters and the exploited) and* The Resistible Rise of Arturo Ui *(a comical parody of Hitler's rise, linking business and fascism).*

He wrote several other famous plays during this period: The Life of Galileo *and* Mother Courage and Her Children, *both warning of Nazism;* The Good Person of Szechuan *with its Marxist message that the good in every person is destroyed by alienation; and* The Caucasian Chalk Circle, *a complicated play within a play where good ultimately triumphs.*

Brecht returned to Berlin in 1948, where he set up a theater ensemble and continued to write while becoming increasingly unhappy about the culturally repressive East German regime. He died of a heart attack in 1956.

German-Argentine composer Mauricio Kagel (*right*) with German sociologist, philosopher, and musicologist Theodor Adorno (*left*).

"All the interests of my reason, speculative as well as practical, combine in the three following questions: 1. What can I know? 2. What ought I to do? 3. What may I hope?"

—Immuanel Kant

After World War I, the Weimar Republic saw the rise of modernist writers. They included Thomas Mann (1875—1955), whose *Buddenbrooks* and *Death in Venice* was highly successful; Herman Hesse (1877—1962), who won the Nobel Prize in 1946; and Franz Kafka (1883—1924), whose works such as *The Trial* and *The Castle* portrayed humanity's powerlessness in modern life.

Many modern German writers explored the guilt and angst of dealing with their Nazi past. Günter Grass (b. 1927) sees the role of a writer as a highly political one. In the 1990s he was one of the few who spoke critically of German reunification. Grass won the Nobel Prize in 1999. Heinrich Böll (1917—85) published his *Billiards at Half-Past Nine* in 1959, the same year as Grass's famous *The Tin Drum*. Eastern German writer Christa Wolf's (b. 1929) *The Quest for Christa T* describes the conflict between historical development and the protagonist's individual claims.

PHILOSOPHY

Germany has produced many profound philosophers, some of whom have had a massive impact on the world as a whole, such as Karl Marx.

THEODOR ADORNO   Theodor Adorno (1903—69) was a German sociologist, philosopher, and musicologist known for his critical theory of society. He coined the term *culture industry*, meaning that popular culture is akin to a factory producing standardized cultural goods—through film, radio, and magazines—to manipulate the masses into passivity. He saw this mass-produced culture as a danger to the high arts. Culture industries may cultivate false needs; that is, needs created and satisfied by capitalism. True needs, in contrast, are freedom, creativity, and genuine happiness.

Adorno wrote and co-authored several influential books, including *Dialectic of Enlightenment* (with Max Horkheimer), *Philosophy of New Music*, *The Authoritarian Personality*, and *Minima Moralia*.

FRIEDRICH ENGELS   Friedrich Engels (1820—95) was a German industrialist, social scientist, author, political theorist, philosopher, and alongside Karl Marx, father of Marxist theory. In 1845 he published *The Condition of the Working Class in England*, based on personal observations and research. In 1848 he coauthored *The Communist Manifesto* with Karl Marx, and later he supported Marx financially so that the latter could conduct research and write *Das Kapital*.

JÜRGEN HABERMAS Jürgen Habermas (b. 1929) is a German sociologist and philosopher in the tradition of critical theory and pragmatism. He is perhaps best known for his theory on the concepts of "communicative rationality" and the "public sphere." Communicative rationality, or communicative reason, is a theory or a set of theories that describes human rationality as a necessary outcome of successful communication. The public sphere is an area in social life where individuals can come together to freely discuss and identify societal problems and through that discussion influence political action.

Ludwig Engelhardt's bronze statues of Karl Marx and Friedrich Engels in the Marx-Engels-Forum public park in Mitte, Berlin.

MARTIN HEIDEGGER Martin Heidegger (1889—1976) was a German philosopher known for his central belief that philosophy, and society as a whole, was preoccupied with what it is that exists.

IMMANUEL KANT Immanuel Kant (1724—1804) argued that human understanding is the source of the general laws of nature that structure all our experience and that human reason gives itself the moral law, which is our basis for belief in God, freedom, and immortality.

KARL MARX Karl Heinrich Marx (1818—83) was a German Jewish philosopher, economist, sociologist, historian, journalist, and revolutionary socialist. His ideas played a significant role in the development of social science and the socialist political movement. Revolutionary socialist governments espousing Marxist concepts took power in a variety of countries in the 20th century, leading to the formation of such socialist states as the Soviet Union in 1922 and the People's Republic of China in 1949.

FRIEDRICH NIETZSCHE Friedrich Nietzsche (1844—1900) was a German philosopher of the late 19th century who challenged the foundations of Christianity and traditional morality. He was interested in the enhancement of individual and cultural health and believed in creativity, power, and the realities of the world we live in, rather than those situated in a world beyond. Central to his philosophy is the idea of "life affirmation," which involves an honest questioning of all doctrines that drain life's expansive energies, however socially prevalent those views might be.

German sacred medieval art, such as the wings of the Wurzach Altarpiece, painted by Hans Multscher in 1437, can be appreciated at the Gemäldegalerie museum in Berlin (Staatliche Museen zu Berlin).

FINE ARTS

There are more than 4,500 museums and art galleries throughout Germany. Exhibitions are partly funded by the government, with some sponsorship from large corporations such as BMW.

Albrecht Dürer (1471—1528), in many ways a Renaissance man, was a talented goldsmith, writer, painter, and graphic artist. He is known today mostly for his woodcuts and engravings. Others, such as Hans Holbein the Elder (c. 1465—1524) and Hans Holbein the Younger (1497—1543), were successful portrait painters, while Lucas Cranach (c. 1472—1553), a friend of Martin Luther, became the official Reformation painter. Caspar David Friedrich (1774—1840) was an outstanding Romantic artist.

The Couple or The Couple in Lace was painted in 1925 by Max Ernst.

The Expressionist movement flourished in the early 20th century until it was banned by the Nazis. Some of the champions of this movement were Ernst Barlach (1870—1938), who showed human suffering in sculptures; painter Wassily Kandinsky (1866—1944), who lived in Munich and developed an abstract color art; and the Swiss artist Paul Klee (1879—1940), who brought the Cubist movement to Germany, developing the abstract movement in Munich. Emil Nolde (1867—1956), a member of the artist society Die Brücke, and Franz Marc (1880—1916), a member of the Blue Rider artist group, introduced expressive colors to modernist paintings. A leading abstract artist was Max Ernst (1891—1976), whose use of collage techniques and Dadaism helped to start the German Surrealism movement after World War I. The works he produced from 1936 to 1938 gave his audience a hint of the horrors of Nazism.

More-recent artists include Joseph Beuys (1921—86), who used action art with social and political dimensions; Georg Baselitz (b. 1938), known for his upside-down work; Markus Lüpertz (b. 1941), who used motifs inspired by

German ideology; Bernd Koberling (b. 1938), who derives her themes from nature; and Rebecca Horn (b. 1944), famous for sculpture "performances." Recent painters who fetch the high prices on the international art market are Anselm Kiefer (b. 1945), whose oil paintings feature controversial themes of recent German history, and Gerhard Richter (b. 1932), who uses a technique of photo overlays and blurs.

ARCHITECTURE

Germany's architecture covers a wide range of styles, from the Gothic-period Cologne Cathedral to the expansive Baroque designs of Potsdam's Sans Souci Palace and the neoclassical shapes of Berlin's Schauspielhaus. Unfortunately much of the old, splendid architecture in the former East Germany was destroyed, not only by Allied bombs during World War II but also by years of neglect that led to the demolition of these buildings for safety reasons.

The Bauhaus style was the creation of German architect Walter Gropius and dominated German architectural styles from 1919 to 1933. The Bauhaus style focused on function, uniting engineering and art.

Built in 1925, the Bauhaus Building in Dessau was designed by Walter Gropius to function as a design school.

Some outstanding contemporary buildings in today's Germany include the BMW Building in Munich, the Stuttgart television tower designed by Fritz Leonhardt, the new Philharmonie in Berlin by Hans Scharoun, and the Gallery of the Twentieth Century by Ludwig Mies van der Rohe.

The Berlin Philharmonic Hall was designed by the German architect Hans Scharoun.

INTERNET LINKS

www.hellomagazine.com/travel/201103185115/germany/car/museums/

A web page with breathtaking pictures of Germany's car museums.

www.bbc.co.uk/programmes/b00wcqms

A three-part series in which Andrew Graham-Dixon explores German art, examining the country's unique national style and 500-year cultural legacy.

www.art-germany.com

A website with thousands of samples of German fine art, from representational to conceptual art.

LEISURE

The beach of Timmendorf Strand on the Baltic Sea island of Timmendorf is always packed with bathers during summer.

GERMANS ENJOY A HIGH STANDARD of living in relation to other countries in the world. It used to be common for families to spend their annual holiday period on a Mediterranean beach. Popular destinations now are Asia, Africa, and North and South America.

Within Germany, families spend their leisure time in a variety of ways and typically belong to several hobby clubs that reflect their interests. Leisure activities in Germany account for about 20 percent of the average person's spending, and leisure has become an important industry. The German Leisure Association researches leisure spending and patterns of behavior and gives out information to the public.

A father and his two children enjoy a cycling tour at the freshwater lake Chiemsee in Bavaria.

11

SPORTS

One in three Germans is a member of a sports club and spends a lot of time training in his or her particular sport. Schools benefit from a government funding program that periodically upgrades their gyms, athletic tracks, swimming pools, and other sports facilities.

Gymnastics has been popular since the 19th century and is now funded by the German Sports Aid Foundation, an organization that is supported by private donations and the lottery and is not run by the government. Whereas the former East Germany used to invest large sums in training athletes, funding is now scarcer in the unified Germany.

Jogging is popular as a cheap and quick sport for those trying to keep fit. For those who prefer swimming, public pools are found in all big and small cities, including several spa pools and the Olympic Pool in Munich.

Handball, volleyball, squash, basketball, and cycling remain popular. There is also an interest in Grand Prix racing; a race in the Eifel Mountains near Heidelberg takes place every year.

SOCCER

Soccer, also referred to as football, is the most popular participatory and spectator sport in Germany. The country has an illustrious soccer tradition. The former West Germany won the World Cup three times—in 1954, 1974, and 1990. It was also runner-up four times, in 1966, 1982, 1986, and 2002.

In 1954 West Germany overcame all odds to beat a Hungarian World Cup team that is still considered by many to be the greatest team ever assembled in soccer history.

In 1974 the West German team was beaten by East Germany in an opening-round match of the World Cup. It was the only time the two Germanys played each other in a competitive game. But legendary stars Franz Beckenbauer, Gerd Müller, Sepp Maier, and Paul Breitner turned the tide for West Germany, winning the championship by beating the Netherlands.

The 1990 team, which beat Argentina, was coached by Beckenbauer. The German team also won the European Championship in 1972, 1980, and 1996.

OLIVER KAHN – THE TITAN OF GERMAN FOOTBALL

Born in Karlsruhe in 1969, German soccer Oliver Rolf Kahn, or "The Titan," as he is commonly referred to, is considered to be one of the best goalkeepers of all time.

He started playing at six in Karlsruher SC, where he carved his niche at goalkeeping, then moved on to Bayern Munich in 1994. Internationally, Kahn has also played in the Fédération Internationale de Football Association (FIFA) World Cups from 1998 to 2006, serving as team captain during the 2002 games.

All in all, this goalkeeping legend has won eight Bundesliga championships, six German Cups, the 1996 Union of European Football Associations (UEFA) Cup, the 2001 UEFA Champions League, and the Intercontinental Cup. He also gained fame with four consecutive UEFA Best European Goalkeeper awards, three International Federation of Football History & Statistics (IFFHS) World's Best Goalkeeper awards, and two German Footballer of the Year trophies. At the 2002 FIFA World Cup, he became the first and only goalkeeper in the tournament's history to receive the Golden Ball, an award for the tournament's best player.

Kahn officially retired from professional soccer in 2008 and received his coaching license in 2010.

Top-league clubs such as Bayern Munich, Borussia Dortmund, and Bayer Leverkusen take part in European competitions, with Bayern being the most successful. Many top players have gone to play in the Spanish and Italian leagues, to pit their skills against other top-class players.

Most Bundesliga (Federal League) games are played on Saturday afternoons, and television excerpts are shown on Saturday evenings.

After the reunification, the former national East and West German teams merged into one. The 2010 World Cup German team reflected the changing demographic of Germany. It was significantly multicultural, as 11 of the players in the 23-man finals roster were eligible to play for other countries, despite 10 of the 11 being born or raised in Germany.

Women hiking along a trail in Reit im Winkl in Bavaria.

THE GREAT OUTDOORS

Germans love to participate in outdoor activities, which they feel brings them closer to the freedom of the hills and forests. Hiking, walking, and rock climbing, particularly in the mountains of southern Germany, are popular pastimes on weekends and vacations.

The traditional Alpine lifestyle of fresh air and healthy food is a part of German folklore. There are well-marked hiking trails in the Alps, and mountain huts provide food and shelter along the way for people on long hikes. Boy Scout trips and outdoor camps in the hills have traditionally been part of the school year. And adventurous mountaineers attempt to scale the Zugspitze or one of the smaller peaks.

Horseback riding is popular, especially in Rhineland-Palatinate, the Neckar Valley, and Franconia. Water sports are also popular: Boating trips are available on the Mosel and Neckar rivers; sailing and windsurfing are practiced on the North and Baltic Seas and on the Mecklenburg Lakes; and canoeing takes place on the Neckar and Lahn rivers and in the Black Forest. In the Bavarian rivers, trout fishing is common. Salmon are found in the Danube. Deep-sea fishing trips can be arranged from Helgoland. Germans must pass a rigorous exam in order to obtain a fishing license.

WINTER SPORTS

Skiing is popular and possible during most winters, as there is usually enough snow. The Alps are the main skiing area, and while most of the accessible slopes and facilities are in neighboring Austria, the sport remains very popular. The town of Garmisch-Partenkirchen is the skiing center of Germany and is extremely popular for weekend trips from Munich and other southern cities. Cross-country skiing is popular in the Bavarian and Thuringian forests,

along with tobogganing, bobsledding, and curling (a game played on ice in which two teams slide curling stones toward a mark in a circle). Ice-skating is another popular sport, especially on the frozen Bavarian lakes and Hamburg's network of waterways.

The country's superb training facilities have helped Germany produce such outstanding winter-sports superstars as skater Katarina Witt, who won numerous championships for the former East Germany, including Olympic gold medals in 1984 and 1988. In the 2002 Winter Olympics at Salt Lake City in the United States, Germany finished on top, with 36 medals. Germany finished second at the 2010 Winter Olympics in Vancouver.

AT HOME

Reading books, magazines, and the country's many local newspapers is a common form of relaxation, along with watching television. Card games are popular, especially bridge and skat.

Do-it-yourself home improvement is an increasingly popular leisure activity. Growing vegetables and flowers in plots, often on the outskirts of towns though sometimes near town centers, is another form of relaxation for many apartment occupants. And of course, the car-loving Germans love to clean, polish, and maintain their vehicles, then drive them to visit friends or explore the countryside.

The most popular German card game is skat, which was developed in the early 19th century. Three players use a pack of 32 cards and start bidding. The winning bidder takes on the other two players and has to win more than half of the available points to win the game.

FORMULA ONE CAR RACING

Michael Schumacher is a German Formula One racing driver for the Mercedes team. While his association with Mercedes has been noteworthy, he is most famous for his 11-year spell with Ferrari. Schumacher is a seven-time World Champion and is widely regarded as one of the greatest F1 drivers of all time. He holds many Formula One records, including most races won in a single season, 13, in 2004. In 2002 he became the only driver in Formula One history to finish in the top three in every race of a season; he then broke the record for most consecutive podium finishes. According to the official Formula One website he is "statistically the greatest driver the sport has ever seen."

Off the track, Schumacher is an ambassador for the United Nations Educational Scientific and Cultural Organization (UNESCO) and a spokesman for driver safety. He has been involved in numerous humanitarian efforts throughout his life and donated tens of millions of dollars to charity. Michael and his younger brother Ralf are the only brothers to win races in Formula One, and they were the first brothers to finish first and second in the same race, in Montreal in 2001, and then again (in switched order) in 2003.

VACATIONS

The generous amount of annual leave from work, as well as school breaks, allows most Germans to take a family vacation for at least two weeks every year. Germans enjoy traveling and exploring different countries—whether it be the beaches of the Mediterranean or faraway places in Asia, Africa, and North America.

Vacationing by the seaside is most popular among Germans, especially for those interested in water sports. Many also enjoy meeting people and sampling the local cuisine of the countries they visit.

Despite the economic slowdown, Germans are still some of the world's greatest tourists, traveling mainly to Austria, Italy, Spain, and the former Yugoslavia, as well as Greece, France, and Mediterranean resorts. There are package tours that cater especially to German tourists, with German food and beer on sale at resorts such as Rimini in Italy and Benidorm in Spain.

Sailing boats on Lake Baldeney in Essen. Sailing is a popular sport in Germany.

Travel restrictions imposed on former East Germans proved frustrating for a people who love to travel and see exotic places. This inherent love for travel may have triggered the first steps of the peaceful revolution of 1989. Within Germany, vacations can be spent visiting the Black Forest, Alpine foothills, inland lakes such as Lake Constance and Chiemsee, and Sylt Island near Denmark.

INTERNET LINKS

http://germanfootballteam.com/

Everything one could want to know about the German national soccer team.

www.skiurlaub-infos.com/173/winter-sports.html

Information about nearly every kind of winter sport there is on the planet.

www.michael-schumacher.de/sites/index.html

A website dedicated to Michael Schumacher, with an option to buy Schumacher merchandise.

Germany is regarded as the birthplace of handball. The first match of the modern era was officially recorded on October 29, 1917, in Berlin. Outdoor handball had its only Olympic Games appearance in the 1936 Berlin Games.

FESTIVALS

The Landshut Wedding Festival is held every few years in Bavaria to remember the wedding of Prince Georg von Wittelbach in 1475. During this festival, which always takes place in summer, people dress in lavish medieval costumes and parade the streets.

GERMANY DOES NOT CELEBRATE any national festivals, not even a national day. Germany does, however, celebrate the reunification of the country on October 3. What it lacks in national festivals, Germany makes up for in regional festivities. Each city and state in Germany celebrates colorful festivals that date back hundreds of years. Many of these festivals have been revived to preserve the local heritage and to boost tourism.

Folk festivals, often with a Christian focus, take place in towns every year, enlivened by traditional entertainment and handicraft stalls. Many pre-Christian rituals have survived in these festivals. For instance, the summer solstice of June 24 is linked to the Feast of Saint John the Baptist, but the practice of rolling burning wheels, which represent the sun's rays, down hills is not Christian.

CARNIVAL

Tied into pre-Christian fertility rites and pagan beliefs, the pre-Lenten carnivals take place mainly in the Catholic areas of Germany. People celebrate by wearing terrifying masks that resemble witches, spirits, and demons, as well as by taking part in costume balls and fancy-dress competitions.

Traditional carnival costumes and uniquely painted and hand-carved wooden masks on display during the pre-Lenten Fastnacht carnival at the Black Forest village in Baden-Württemberg.

One of the more famous carnivals takes place in Cologne, where local associations elect three people to dress up as the Carnival Prince, the Peasant, and the Virgin for the duration of the carnival. These characters, usually portrayed by middle-aged businesspeople, wear costumes and throw toffees at the crowd from their privileged positions in the major parades.

Cologne's carnival starts at precisely 11:11 A.M. on November 11 but gets into full swing during the *Tolle Tage* (TOLL-eh TAHG-eh), or Crazy Days, just before Lent. The Thursday before Lent is known as Women's Day. On this day, women cut off the neckties of any men within reach.

On the Sunday before Lent a big informal procession takes place. The highlight of the carnival is Rose Monday, or Rosenmontag, when another large procession takes place. The procession includes a jester's speech with funny references to local and national politics. Local songs are sung by the crowd as the procession goes by. As there have consistently been more than one million spectators on the streets for the Rose Monday parade every year, the Cologne carnival is one of the largest street festivals in Europe. Ash Wednesday marks the beginning of Lent, a period of 46 days of fasting and discipline before Easter.

Munich's carnival has a young couple, dressed as the Prinz (Prince) and Prinzessin (Princess). They take part in a stylish procession that includes a dance on Shrove Tuesday, in which the women of the fruit-and-vegetable market perform a dance.

In the town of Elzach in southern Germany's Black Forest, masked "fools" run through the town wearing large decorated hats and hitting people with blown-up hogs' bladders. In Rottweil rival groups of "fools" jump through the town's Black Gate at 8:00 A.M. Meanwhile, jesters' banquets are held in Stockach and Grosselfingen, as well as in Lindau on Lake Constance.

THE MUNICH OKTOBERFEST

Every year since 1810, there has been a beer-drinking festival in Munich. The Oktoberfest began as a horserace held in honor of the marriage of Bavaria's Crown Prince Ludwig I and Princess Therese von Sachsen-Hildburghausen of Saxony.

In subsequent years, the race was combined with the state agricultural fair, and booths serving food and drinks were introduced. By the 20th century, these booths had developed into large beer halls.

Today Oktoberfest lasts 16 days; it starts in September, as the weather is warmer then, and ends on the first Sunday of October. The festival is internationally famous and attracts tourists from every corner of the world. The central attraction is the huge beer tents where one can drink beer from quarter-gallon (1-liter) glasses. After a couple of these, people will jump on the benches and tables and sing traditional drinking songs while waitresses bustle among the long tables bringing additional drinks. Outside the beer tents, there are sideshows, a funfair, trinket stalls, and musical performances as well as a range of traditional food stalls.

During the Oktoberfest, the beer tents in Munich are filled with hundreds of people.

OTHER DRINKING FESTIVALS

Some regions have their own festivals to celebrate successful harvests. During Stuttgart's Volksfest, a harvest festival, up to 1.5 million gallons (5.68 million l) of beer and 300,000 chickens are consumed. The festival has been held each year since 1840. In Erlangen, the Bergkirchweih Festival starts on the Thursday before Pentecost and lasts for 12 days. Beer sampling and brass bands add to the fun.

Gingerbread houses and other festive decorations on sale during Christmas season in Germany.

Various wine festivals are enjoyed in the Rhineland. In November winemakers will place brooms outside their doors as a signal that their wine is ready. They then turn their homes into drinking places for the next couple of months.

CHRISTIAN FESTIVALS

Epiphany on January 6 is a public holiday in the Roman Catholic states. In the countryside, children dress up as the three kings, with the letters *C* (for Caspar), *M* (Melchior), or *B* (Balthasar) sewn onto their costumes.

Good Friday is a public holiday, and many Christians fast or do not eat meat that day. On Easter Sunday, children search for the Easter Hare and eat decorated hard-boiled eggs. Easter Monday is the time for egg-rolling competitions.

Ascension Day is a public holiday throughout Germany, and processions and the blessing of crops are held. Corpus Christi is celebrated only in Catholic areas, with elaborate altars and pictures made of flower petals placed along roads and processions.

The last day of October is the Protestant celebration of Reformation Day. November 1 (All Saints' Day) and November 2 (All Souls' Day) are times for tidying church graveyards and laying new wreaths. November 10 is Saint Martin's Day, when Protestant churches hold celebrations honoring Martin Luther and Catholics honor a saint with the same name.

Christmas celebrations are family affairs. On December 5, children leave shoes outside their rooms to be filled by Saint Nicholas. Families put an advent wreath on the table and decorate their homes with fir branches, while children open advent calendars every morning from December 1 until December 24, Christmas Eve.

On the fourth Sunday before Christmas Eve, the traditional Christmas markets open in town squares throughout Germany. Decorations as well as goodies for family celebrations can be bought there. The most famous

Christmas market takes place in Nuremberg, where the local delicacy is a type of gingerbread called Nuremberg *lebkuchen* (LEH-p-KOO-hen). A popular drink to be enjoyed on the cold days is *gluehwein* (GLOO-vine), or mulled wine. The main celebrations take place on Christmas Eve, rather than Christmas Day. The tree is decorated on Christmas Eve, after which many Germans attend a special midnight service in church.

PROCESSIONS

Mounted processions are held during religious celebrations. The Kötztinger Pfingstritt on Whit Monday involves 500 costumed horses and riders riding four miles (6.4 km) to an open-air Mass. A festival that remembers the death of Jesus Christ is celebrated with mounted processions in Bad Wurzach and Weingarten. Other celebrations that involve horse riding take place to honor particular Catholic saints.

OTHER FESTIVALS

During Bleigiessen on New Year's Eve, Germans celebrate a ritual that dates from pre-Christian times: They pour hot lead into cold water and try to look into the future.

Horse festivals are popular in northern Germany. They generally take place around Pentecost and include medieval-era contests such as jousting. During festivals in Kiel and Dithmarschen, competitors try to stay on a wooden figure turned on an axis called Roland's Riding.

Shooting festivals take place from May to August. The largest of these festivals, held in Hannover in July, lasts 10 days and has more than 5,000 competitors. Another such festival, Shepherds' Run, is held annually on the last weekend in August in the town of Markgröningen near Stuttgart. On the Friday, spectators can catch a glimpse of the life of a shepherd by watching the sheepherding contest, in which shepherds compete at tasks in

Close to 950 riders and horses takes part at the annual religious Kötztinger Pfingstritt procession in Germany.

There is now a Bleigiessen kit sold in supermarkets that makes it easy for Germans to enact this ritual.

OBERAMMERGAU PASSION PLAYS

In 1633 an outbreak of the plague wiped out many villages in the Bavarian Alps. As the plague approached the village of Oberammergau, the villagers prayed to God and made a promise to perform a passion play every 10 years if only they were spared. Miraculously the plague stopped short of the village. In 1634 the Oberammergau passion play was staged for the first time. In 1700 it was decided that the play would be performed in years ending in "0"; exceptions were made in 1934, to mark the play's 300th anniversary, and in 1984, to celebrate the play's 350th anniversary.

Since then, every 10 years—the next performance will be in the year 2020—the play is performed by a cast of local amateur actors and actresses and countless extras, from May to September. Thousands of Christians, theatergoers, and tourists flock to this tiny mountain hamlet to watch the two-day-long reenactment of Christ's life and death on the cross.

Over the years the play has developed to include passages from the Old Testament in addition to the life of Jesus Christ. In 1970 the script was arranged in such a way as to not place the blame of Christ's death on the Jews. In 2000 the rule of hiring only Christian performers was lifted, and for the first time, non-Christian townspeople were allowed to perform in the play.

The venue of the play is a modern structure that can seat up to 4,800 people. The audience faces an open stage that is reputedly the largest open-air stage in the world. The outside walls of many homes in Oberammergau are decorated with beautiful paintings depicting the death and resurrection of Christ.

the Markgröningen fields. The actual "shepherds' run," the centerpiece of the festival, takes place on the Saturday. First shepherds' daughters and trained female shepherds, dressed prettily in red, white, and green skirts, then male shepherds race barefoot over a stubble field 300 paces long. The winners receive a sheep as a prize and are crowned Shepherd Queen and Shepherd King.

The Tanzelfest in the Allgäu is one of many medieval celebrations in Germany. It lasts for 10 days, and people dressed in historical costumes take part in traditional dances. A reenactment of the Pied Piper legend is held annually in the town of Hamlin (Hameln in German). Some Germans celebrate Walpurgis Night on April 30, believing that witches and the devil congregate in the Harz Mountains that evening. In autumn the Rhineland in Flames festival holds firework displays.

Labor Day is celebrated on May 1, and the penultimate Sunday in November is Remembrance Day.

A procession during the Tanzelfest in Allgäu.

INTERNET LINKS

www.oktoberfest.de/en/

Everything one would want to know about Munich's Oktoberfest, from its history to how it is currently being staged, complete with live web telecasts of the events and an iPhone app available for download.

www.oberammergau-passion.com/en-gb/home/home.html

The official website of the Oberammergau Passion Play, complete with a welcome from the town's mayor.

www.koelnerkarneval.de/en/cologne-carnival/

A comprehensive site about the Cologne Carnival, including photos available for download and the history of the carnival.

The Virgin in the Passion Play is traditionally acted by a man. Beards and moustaches are forbidden for this role. From 1936 to 1943, the Virgin was ordered by Nazi authorities to be played by a real woman.

FOOD

A food display in a gourmet delicatessen in Bremen. The sheer variety of meats and sausages found in Germany is sure to satisfy any taste buds.

GERMANY HAS A RICH VARIETY of food and drink, much of which is grown or produced at home. A combination of richly spiced meats and salted fish, accompanied by vegetables and washed down with wine or beer, is the typical German's hearty meal.

Because most Germans traditionally worked in the fields, they needed a diet rich in protein. Thus the country's traditional cuisine revolves around red meat and potatoes. However, there is now an increasing number of vegetarian restaurants throughout the country.

Diners in a *Ratskeller* in Bavaria. A *Ratskeller* refers to a bar or restaurant located in the basement, either at or near the city hall.

German regional cuisine can be divided into many varieties, including Bavarian (southern Germany), Thuringian (central Germany), and Lower Saxon (Saxony-Anhalt). East German cuisine was strongly influenced by Russia, Hungary, Bulgaria, and other East European countries from the 1960s onward.

Nearly 600 types of freshly baked bread, or *brot*, is available throughout Germany.

In different regions, the same food may come in different styles. For example, a Bavarian dish may be prepared differently in Schleswig-Holstein.

LOCAL SPECIALTIES

Wurst, or German sausage, is the most prominent item of German cuisine. There are more than 1,200 types of wurst, often made from veal, pork, mustard, spices, and curries. Each region has its own type of sausage, like the Bavarian white sausage, *weisswurst* (VYES-vurst), with parsley and onion, or the grilled chipolata.

Blood pudding, poultry cutlets coated with crumbs, cuts of beef and venison, smoked and pickled herring from the North Sea, sauerkraut (pickled cabbage), a potato salad called *kartoffelsalat* (kar-TOFF-el-sahl-AHT), spiced red cabbage, and mushrooms are found throughout the country, prepared in different ways.

A rich selection of breads, or *brot*, is served in restaurants and bought daily in bakeries. Many love the dark rye pumpernickel breads.

Wine-producing areas such as Baden-Württemberg, Mosel, Franconia, and Bavaria are particularly famous for their good food. Local specialties include eel, plum, and vegetable soup, and fresh herrings in Hamburg; *hoppel poppel* (HOP-pel POP-pel), a potato-and-ham omelet, in Berlin; suckling pig and roast knuckle of pork in Bavaria; ham eaten with pumpernickel bread in Westphalia; boiled or breaded fried fish, particularly catfish from the Danube, near Passau; numerous varieties of sausage in Nuremberg; and green herb sauce with pork chops or beef in Frankfurt.

Other favorite foods include Bavarian flour dumplings called *knödel* (K-NOO-dell) and Swabian noodles called *spätzle* (or spaetzle), which resemble Italian flat noodles, served with meat or vegetables. Pickled radish from Bavaria is a popular accompaniment to beer.

Hazelnuts have been used in Germany for more than 11,000 years, according to archaeological pollen studies.

MEALS

Families have breakfast at around 7 A.M., or even earlier, in order for the children to be at school and adults at work by 8 A.M. The typical German full breakfast includes a variety of breads, sausages, and salami and other cold meats, along with cheeses and perhaps some jam for a sweet taste, washed down with coffee, tea, or fruit juice. On a daily basis, however, most families simply have fresh rolls, jam and butter, and coffee or tea.

Lunch, the main meal of the day, is eaten between 11:30 A.M. and 2:00 P.M. and consists of a cooked meal with vegetables. Working people usually have a hot meal at the office cafeteria or a nearby restaurant or, if pressed for time, a hot pastry filled with cheese or sausages. Most schoolchildren have lunch at home after school.

The evening meal is generally quite light. In the south, it may consist of a hot meal of sausage, some potato salad, and soup; in the north, it might be cheese, cold meats, and salad. An early evening meal allows people time to pursue a variety of leisure activities.

A store at the Viktualienmarkt, a daily food market, in Munich. While originally a farmers' market, the site now draws many gourmet food sellers and buyers.

Founded in 1803 by a tavern owner, Krombacher Brauerei in Kreuztal, Siegen-Wittgenstein, was ranked Germany's second-best-selling beer company (after Oettinger Brauerei) by *Bild* newspaper in 2010.

EATING OUT

It is easy to find good food in Germany. Restaurants, taverns, and beer gardens offer delicious food. Generally the menu is displayed on a small blackboard outside the entrance.

Due to the large number of foreign residents in Germany, Germans can choose from a wide variety of international cuisines, such as Italian, Spanish, Greek, Turkish, and Yugoslav. French food, although expensive, has become very popular among the upper class. There are also many local bakeries, called *Bäckerei* (Baker-HI), and fast-food restaurants. Budget meals are available at some butchers, called *Metzger* (METS-ger), and department stores.

ALCOHOL

Red wine has always been hard to produce in the German climate, which accounts for the domination of white wine.

Germany produces much of its own wine, generally in the Rhineland area. The total wine production is usually around 1.2 billion bottles annually, which places Germany as the eighth-largest wine-producing country in the world. White wine accounts for almost two-thirds of the production.

Wines are categorized into table wines, quality wines, and prime-quality wines and are priced accordingly. There are also young wines such as *Federweisser* (FAY-der-vye-sser), and sparkling wines, called *Sekt* (SEKT). Wine is not taxed in Germany.

Beer is not only the Germans' favorite drink, but it is also a major industry. Germany has 1,300 breweries and 5,000 varieties of beer.

THE REINHEITSGEBOT The German beer industry has been heavily regulated since the 16th century, in order to ensure that all beer produced retained a high-quality standard. A Bavarian government decree of 1516—the Reinheitsgebot, or Purity Law—declared that beer should contain only malt, hops, yeast, barley, and water. This standard has been adopted throughout Germany over the centuries as a guarantee of superior taste and quality. Germany also produces a wide range of nonalcoholic beers. The revised Reinheitsgebot of 1993 allows yeast to be used for bottom-fermented beer as well, and for different kinds of malt, as well as sugar, to be used for top-fermented beer. All ingredients and the process itself are subject to additional regulations.

Friends enjoying refreshing steins of beer in Bavaria.

Since Germany is a member of the European Union, beers from other member countries—which many Germans feel are not comparable to German brands, as they do not comply with the Purity Law—are now allowed to be sold in the country. Interestingly, beer consumption is on the decline in Germany.

INTERNET LINKS

www.travelsthroughgermany.com/website2/germanfood.htm

Offering a wealth of German food recipes.

http://allrecipes.com/howto/german-cuisine/

Has an overview of German cuisine and links to numerous mouth-watering recipes (click on "German Recipe Collection").

www.germanfoodguide.com/cooking.htm

A guide to German cuisine that divides German food into its individual regional specialties.

Beer is the world's third-most-popular thirst quencher, after water and tea. The Germans are behind only the Czechs and the Irish in their per-capita consumption of beer—29.06 gallons (110 l) per person in 2011.

SAUERBRATEN (SOUR ROAST)

This hearty dish originated in Rhineland. This recipe serves eight to 10 people.

2 ¹/₂ pounds (1.13 kg) beef brisket

4 cups (1 l) water

1 cup (250 ml) red-wine vinegar

2 bay leaves

1 clove

4 peppercorns

2 allspice berries

1 medium carrot (peeled and sliced)

1 piece celery root (if available)

1 piece parsley root (if available)

4 tablespoons (60ml) oil or margarine

¹/₂ cup (125 ml) sour cream

1 ¹/₂ tablespoons (22.5 ml) cornstarch

Salt and pepper

Place meat in a deep saucepan. Fill saucepan with mixture of water and vinegar until meat is covered. Add bay leaves, clove, peppercorns, allspice, carrot, and celery and parsley roots. Refrigerate saucepan for two or three days, turning the meat over once a day. Heat oil or margarine in a frying pan, then brown meat on all sides. Add salt and another ¹/₂ cup of water. Cover pot and simmer for 1 ¹/₂ hours on low heat, making sure there is always some liquid; if not, add 1 or 2 tablespoons of water. Remove the meat from the pot, leaving the liquid in the pot. Mix the sour cream with the cornstarch, making sure there are no lumps, and stir into the pot. Bring the mixture to a boil, then remove from heat. Add salt and pepper to taste. Cut the meat into serving slices, pour the mixture over it, and serve with potato dumplings or noodles, and boiled vegetables.

BAVARIAN VANILLA CREAM

A simple and delightful dessert from Bavaria. This recipe serves six to eight people.

3 cups (750 ml) milk

1 vanilla pod

4 tablespoons (60 ml) gelatin, unflavored

1/2 cup (125 ml) cold water

4 egg yolks

1/2 cup (125 ml) sugar

1 cup (250 ml) heavy cream, whipped

Pour milk into a saucepan. Slit vanilla pod, and scrape the seeds into the milk, finally adding the pod itself to the milk as well. Leave for 30 minutes. In another saucepan, add gelatin to the cold water. Heat the mixture to dissolve the gelatin completely. Then heat the milk in the saucepan, bringing it to a boil. Beat the egg yolks with sugar until creamy and slowly add into the boiling milk. Remove from heat. While the milk mixture is still hot, pour it in the dissolved gelatin. Cool until slightly thickened. Slowly stir in the whipped cream. Pour into a fancy mold or individual parfait glasses. Chill in the refrigerator for at least six hours. Unmold carefully, and decorate with fresh fruits, such as berries, mint leaves, and syrup.

*Other options: Bavarian Vanilla Cream can be eaten alone or used as a filling for molded cakes, pies, and cold charlottes. This last dessert is made by lining the border of a mold with ladyfinger cookies and filling the center with cream. To make a Bavarian pie, simply add the Bavarian Vanilla Cream to a cooled pie shell or crust, and chill in the refrigerator.

MAP OF GERMANY

Aachen, A3
Augsburg, C4

Baden-Baden, B4
Baden-Württemberg, B4—B5
Baltic Sea, C1, D1
Bamberg, C4
Bavaria, B3—B5, C3—C5
Bavarian Alps, C5
Bavarian Forest, C4, D4
Bayreuth, C4
Berchtesgaden Alps, C5
Berlin, C2
Black Forest, B4—B5
Bonn, B3
Brandenburg, C2—C3, D2—D3
Bremen, B2
Brunswick, C2

Chiemsee, Lake, C5
Cologne, A3
Constance, Lake, B5

Dachau, C4
Danube River, B4—B5, C4
Dresden, D3
Düsseldorf, A3

East Frisian Islands, A2, B2
Eifel Mountains, A3
Eisenach, B3
Elbe River, B2, C2—C3, D3
Emden, B2
Erzgebirge Range, C3

Essen, B3
Frankfurt, B3
Freising, C4

Garmisch-Partenkirchen, C5

Hamburg, B2
Hannover, B2
Harz Range, C3
Heidelberg, B4
Helgoland, B1
Hesse, B3—B4
Hunsrück Mountains, A4, B4

Inn River, C4—C5
Isar River, C4—C5

Jena, C3

Karlsruhe, B4
Kiel, B1
Kiel Bay, B1, C1
Koblenz, B3

Lahn River, B3
Lausatia (region), D3
Lech River, C4—C5
Leipzig, C3
Lower Saxony, B2
Lüneburger Heath, B2

Magdeburg, C2
Main River, B3—B4, C3—C4
Mannheim, B4
Mecklenburg, C2
Mecklenburg Bay, C1
Mecklenburg-Vorpommern, C1—C2, D1—D2

Mosel River, A4, B3
Munich, C4
Münster, B2

Neckar River, B4
Neckar Valley, B4
Neisse River, D2—D3
Nord-Ostsee Canal, B1
North Rhine-Westphalia, A2—A3, B2—B3
North Sea, A1—A2, B1—B2
North Frisian Islands, B1
Nuremberg, C4

Oberammergau, C5
Oder River, C2, D2

Passau, C4
Potsdam, C2

Rhine River, B3—B4
Rhineland-Palatinate, A3—A4, B3—B4
Ruhr Industrial Area, A3
Ruhr River, A3, B3

Saarland, A4, B4
Saxony, C3—D3
Saxony-Anhalt, C2—C3
Schaal, Lake, C2
Schleswig-Holstein, B1—B2, C1—C2
Solingen, B3
Starnberg, C5
Starnbergsee See, C5
Straubing, C4
Stuttgart, B4
Sylt, B1

Taunus Mountains, B3
Thuringia, B3, C3
Titisee, Lake, B5

Vogelsberg Mountains, B3

Weimar, C3
Weser River, B2—B3
Westerwald, B3
Wilhelmshaven, B2

Zugspitze, C5

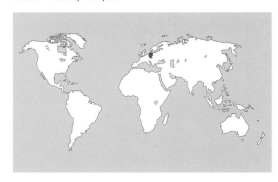

ECONOMIC GERMANY

Agriculture

 Barley

 Potatoes

 Vegetables

 Wheat

 Wine

Manufacturing

 Aircraft

 Chemicals

 Electronics

 Food products

 Jewelry

 Machinery

 Musical instruments

 Oil refinery

 Ship making

 Vehicles

Natural Resources

 Coal

 Fish

 Natural gas

 Oil

 Steel and other metals

Services

 Port

ABOUT THE ECONOMY

OVERVIEW

Germany is the world's fourth-largest economy and a major industrial and technological power. Deriving its wealth from manufacturing and trade, Germany continues to be the most economically influential country in the EU, despite the effects of the debt crisis. However, Germany's status as "eurozone's anchor of stability" and its AAA credit rating has been threatened by a possible exit of Greece from the eurozone and the prospect of Germany having to support the other struggling eurozone countries.

GROSS DOMESTIC PRODUCT (GDP)

$3.1 trillion (2012 estimate)

CURRENCY

The euro (EUR) replaced the deutsche mark (DM) in 2002 at a fixed rate of 1.95583 marks per euro.
€1 = 123 cents
$1 = EUR 82 cents (2012 estimate)
Notes: 5, 10, 20, 50, 100, 200, 500 euros
Coins: 1, 2, 5, 10, 20, 50 cents; 1, 2 euros

GDP SECTORS

Agriculture 0.8 percent, industry 28.6 percent, services 70.6 percent (2012 estimate)

WORKFORCE

43.62 million (2011 estimate)

UNEMPLOYMENT RATE

6.5 percent (2012 estimate)

AGRICULTURAL PRODUCTS

Potatoes, wheat, barley, sugar beets, fruit, cabbages, cattle, pigs, poultry

INDUSTRIAL PRODUCTS

Iron, steel, coal, cement, chemicals, machinery, vehicles, machine tools, electronics, food and beverages, and ships

MAJOR EXPORTS

Automobiles, machinery, chemicals, computer and electronic products, electrical equipment, pharmaceuticals, metals, transport equipment, and foodstuffs

MAJOR IMPORTS

Machinery, data processing equipment, vehicles, chemicals, oil and gas, metals, electric equipment, pharmaceuticals, foodstuffs, and agricultural products

MAJOR TRADE PARTNERS

France, the United States, the Netherlands, UK, Italy, China, Austria, Belgium, and Switzerland

MAJOR PORTS

Bremen, Bremerhaven, Brunsbuttel, Duisburg, Emden, Frankfurt, Hamburg, Kiel, Luebeck, and Rostock

CULTURAL GERMANY

Rothenburg
The town has managed to retain its 16th-century feel, with cobbled streets, quaint old houses, fountains, and charming back alleys. The architecture of its public buildings, such as the town hall, is a mixture of Gothic and Renaissance styles.

Cologne Cathedral
A superb example of Gothic architecture, the cathedral was begun in 1248 but completed only in 1880. Its rising towers, detailed sculptures, and impressive stained-glass windows reflect the wealth of the city during the Renaissance and the exquisite local craftsmanship.

Bamberg
Founded in the 10th century, this city's charming architecture retains elements of both Gothic and Romanesque styles. The cathedral, built in Gothic style, and the sculpture of the Bamberg Horseman are two of the city's most important attractions.

Rhine River
Boat rides along romantic castles, vineyards, and picturesque towns are popular among local and foreign tourists.

Black Forest
A favorite holiday spot, the forest is popular with tourists because of its spas; beautiful mountain scenery; large lakes, such as the Titisee; and rivers, where canoeing can be enjoyed. Towns in the forest are also popular for their well-preserved Gothic architecture and cuckoo clock industry.

Alps
The Alps of southern Germany on the border with Austria are a favorite winter holiday spot for skiing and snowboarding.

Passion Plays
Every ten years, the town of Oberammergau hosts a series of plays reenacting the last days of Christ's life and his resurrection. Performed by the townspeople for the first time in 1634 as an offering of thanks to God for sparing the town from the plague, the plays are now held on a huge open-air stage.

Dresden
Modeled after Versailles, the Zwinger was built by Elector Augustus of Saxony in 1719. A collection of Baroque-style buildings, most of these have now been converted into museums. Formal gardens, beautiful fountains adorned with sculptures of mythical figures, and connecting pavilions in the surrounding areas add to the grandeur of the palace.

Berlin Wall
Built in 1961 by the government of East Berlin to keep its citizens from fleeing to West Berlin, it was opened in 1989 after swift social and political reforms within East Germany. The wall was finally torn down in 1990, but some parts of it have been uprooted and are now exhibited in a museum in Berlin.

Bayreuth Music Festival
Since 1882, the Richard Wagner festival has been held every year for one month, from July to August, in the Festspielhaus in Bayreuth. Only Wagner's operas are performed during the festival.

Nuremberg
The walled Old Town in the city retains much of its Renaissance charm, with its castle, museum, old houses, and fortifications. German artist Albrecht Dürer's house has been preserved as a museum.

Neuschwanstein Castle
Built by the eccentric King Louis II of Bavaria in 1886, the fairy-tale-like castle was designed by a theater stage decorator. A great admirer of the composer Richard Wagner, the king had the walls of the castle decorated with scenes from Wagner's operas.

OFFICIAL NAME
Federal Republic of Germany

DESCRIPTION OF NATIONAL FLAG
Three horizontal bands: black, red, and gold

NATIONAL ANTHEM
"Das Lied der Deutschen." Text by August Heinrich Hoffmann von Fallersleben, melody by Franz Joseph Haydn, originally written for Kaiser Franz II

CAPITAL
Berlin

STATES
Baden-Württemberg, Bavaria, Berlin, Brandenburg, Bremen, Hamburg, Hesse, Lower Saxony, Mecklenburg-Vorpommern, North Rhine-Westphalia, Rhineland-Palatinate, Saarland, Saxony, Saxony-Anhalt, Schleswig-Holstein, Thuringia

POPULATION
81.2 million (2013 estimate)

OFFICIAL LANGUAGE
German

LITERACY RATE
99 percent

ETHNIC GROUPS
German 91.5 percent, Turkish 2.4 percent, Greek, Italian, Polish, Russian, Spanish, Serbo-Croatian, and others 6.1 percent

RELIGIONS
Protestant 34 percent, Roman Catholic 34 percent, Muslim 3.7 percent, other or unaffiliated 28.3 percent

LEADERS IN THE ARTS
Albrecht Dürer (1471—1528), Johann Sebastian Bach (1685—1750), George Handel (1685—1759), Johann Wolfgang von Goethe (1749—1832), Ludwig van Beethoven (1770—1827), Thomas Mann (1875—1955), Hesse (1877—1962), Walter Gropius (1883—1969), Bertolt Brecht (1898—1956), Günter Grass (b. 1927), Werner Herzog (b. 1942)

LEADERS IN POLITICS
Konrad Adenauer—chancellor of West Germany 1949—63, Erich Honecker—leader of East German SED 1971—90, Helmut Kohl—chancellor of West Germany 1982—90, chancellor of reunited Germany 1990—98, Gerhard Schroeder—chancellor of Germany 1998—2005, Angela Merkel—chancellor of Germany since 2005

TIMELINE

IN GERMANY	IN THE WORLD

A.D. 800
Charlemagne crowned emperor in Rome
870
Formation of the duchies of Franconia, Saxony, Bavaria, and Swabia.
900
Formation of the Duchy of Lorraine
1138–1254
Hohenstaufen dynasty reigns
1235
Emperor Frederick II proclaims the Peace of Mainz, the first imperial law in German.
1517
Martin Luther writes *The Ninety-Five Theses*; the Reformation begins.
1555
The Peace of Augsburg
1618
Thirty Years' War begins
1701
Frederick III of Brandenburg crowns himself king of Prussia
1815
Founding of the German Confederation
1862
Otto von Bismarck becomes prime minister of Prussia
1871
Founding of the German Empire; Bismarck becomes first chancellor of Germany.
1914
Germany joins World War I on the side of Austria.
1918
End of the German monarchy; declaration of a republic by the Social Democrats.
1919
Paris Peace Conference held between France and Great Britain and defeated Germany; Treaty of Versailles signed; election of a national assembly in Weimar.
1923
Raging inflation; attempted coups by right-wing and left-wing radical groups.
1933
Adolf Hitler becomes chancellor
1939
Germany attacks Poland; World War II begins

1206–1368
Genghis Khan unifies the Mongols and starts conquest of the world. At its height, the Mongol Empire under Kublai Khan stretches from China to Persia and parts of Europe and Russia.

1776
U.S. Declaration of Independence
1789–99
The French Revolution

1914
World War I begins

1939
World War II begins

IN GERMANY		IN THE WORLD
1945 Hitler commits suicide; Germany surrenders.		**1945** The United States drops atomic bombs on Hiroshima and Nagasaki. World War II ends.
1948–49 Blockade of West Berlin by the Soviet Union; formation of the Federal Republic of Germany and the German Democratic Republic.		
1961 The government of East Germany builds the Berlin Wall.		
1989 Opening of the Berlin Wall		
1990 Unification treaty signed; Chancellor Kohl becomes first chancellor of unified Germany.		
1992 Treaty on European Union signed		**2001** Terrorists crash planes into New York, Washington D.C., and Pennsylvania.
2002 The euro becomes Germany's official currency.		
2003 Constitutional court decides not to uphold government request to ban neo-Nazi National Democratic Party.		**2003** War in Iraq begins
2004 Opposition CDU-backed candidate Horst Koehler, former IMF head, is elected president.		**2004** Eleven Asian countries are hit by giant tsunami, killing at least 225,000 people.
2005 Parliament ratifies EU constitution; Angela Merkel of the CDU becomes chancellor in a "grand coalition" involving the CDU and the SPD.		**2005** Hurricane Katrina devastates the Gulf Coast of the United States.
2006 Unemployment falls below 4 million for the first time in four years.		
2008 Germany is declared to be in recession.		**2008** Earthquake in Sichuan, China, kills 67,000.
2009 The country is declared out of recession.		**2009** Outbreak of flu virus H1N1 around the world
2011 German government says that all nuclear power plants will be phased out by 2022.		**2011** Twin earthquake and tsunami disasters strike northeast Japan, leaving more than 14,000 dead and thousands more missing.
2012 President Christian Wulff resigns in a corruption scandal. Joachim Gauck is Germany's new president.		**2012** Hurricane Sandy devastates the northeastern United States.

GLOSSARY

Abitur (AH-bee-toor)
Preuniversity exam.

Bundesrat
The house of the federal parliament made up of representatives nominated by the state governments.

Bundestag
The house of the federal parliament elected by citizens.

Cold War
The military and economic rivalry between the capitalist and democratic United States and its allies and the communist Soviet Union and its allies from 1945 to the late 1980s.

confirmation
A religious ceremony practiced by Catholics and Protestants in which a youth is accepted as an adult member of the church.

conurbation
A predominantly urban region including adjacent towns and suburbs; a metropolitan area.

first communion
A religious ceremony practiced by Roman Catholics in which a child takes consecrated bread and wine, as the body and blood of Christ, for the first time.

Gastarbeiter (GAST-ahr-byte-er)
Immigrant worker, literally "guest worker," a term used from the 1960s until the 1980s. Current usage: "migrant worker."

glasnost
The policy of openly discussing economic and social problems in the Soviet Union that was started by Mikhail Gorbachev in the 1980s.

Grundschule (GROONT-shoo-leh)
Elementary school, which German children enter at the age of 6 and attend for the next four or five years.

Gymnasium
Secondary school that prepares students for the preuniversity exam.

Hauptschule (HOWPT-shoo-leh)
Intermediate school that prepares students for admission to a part-time vocational school.

Holy Roman Empire of German Nations
The first German empire, formed from Christian Central European tribes under Charlemagne in A.D. 800, which lasted until 1806.

kaiser
Head of the German empire.

Land (LAHND)
Individual federal state within Germany.

Realschule (RAY-ahl-shoo-leh)
Intermediate school that prepares students for admission to a full-time technical school.

FOR FURTHER INFORMATION

BOOKS

Di Duca, Marc, Anthony Haywood, and Andrea Schulte-Peevers. *Lonely Planet Discover Germany.* Oakland, CA: Lonely Planet, 2010.

Egert-Romanowskiej, Joanna, and Malgorzata Omilanowska. *Germany* (Eyewitness Travel Guides). New York: DK Travel, 2010.

Luthardt, Ernst-Otto. *Journey Through Germany*, 3rd ed. (Journey Through Series). Würzburg: Verlagshaus Würzburg, 2011.

Parmele, Mary Platt. *The Evolution of an Empire: A Brief Historical Sketch of Germany.* Charleston, SC: Nabu Press, 2010.

Somers, Steven. *Those Crazy Germans! A Lighthearted Guide to Germany.* Bloomington, IN: Xlibris Corporation, 2008.

Swick, Edward. *The Everything Learning German Book: Speak, Write, and Understand Basic German in No Time,* 2nd ed. (Everything Series). Avon, MA: Adams Media, 2009.

Winder, Simon. *Germania: In Wayward Pursuit of the Germans and Their History.* New York: Farrar, Straus, and Giroux, March 2010.

DVDS/FILMS

Best of Europe: Beautiful Germany (Blu-ray). Small World Productions, Questar, 2010.

A Musical Journey: Germany—Bavaria. Naxos of America DVD, 2009.

Rise and Fall of Nazi Germany. Columbia River, 2011

MUSIC

Made in Germany: Nena. 101 Distribution, 2009.

Made in Germany: Rammstein. Universal Music, 2011.

Weimar Germany (Time Traveller). Emi Classics, April 2012.

WEBSITES

BBC News: Germany Country Profile. http://news.bbc.co.uk/2/hi/europe/country_profiles/1047864.stm

Federal Ministry of Economics and Technology. www.bmwi.de/English/Navigation/root.html

Federal Statistical Office. https://www.destatis.de/EN/Homepage.html

German—American Heritage Museum. www.ugac.org/gahm/gahm.html

German History for Kids: German Environment. www.historyforkids.org/learn/germans/environment/index.htm

German Life Magazine. www.germanlife.com

Goethe Institut. www.goethe.de/enindex.htm

BIBLIOGRAPHY

BOOKS

Applebaum, Anne. *Iron Curtain: The Crushing of Eastern Europe, 1944—1956*. NY: Doubleday, 2012.

Buckley, William F. *The Fall of the Berlin Wall*. NY: Wiley, 2009.

Fulbrook, Mary. *A Concise History of Germany*, 2nd edition. Cambridge, England: Cambridge University Press, 2008.

Lapavitsas, Costas. *Crisis in the Eurozone*. NY: Verso Books, 2012.

Showalter, Dennis. *The Wars of German Unification*. NY: Bloomsbury, 2004.

WEBSITES

Art Germany. www.art-germany.com

BBC Four: Art of Germany. www.bbc.co.uk/programmes/b00wcqms

BBC Languages: German. www.bbc.co.uk/languages/german/

Destination Germany. www.germany.travel/en/index.html

Deutschland.de: Religious Persuasions. www.deutschland.de/en/religion/religious-persuasions.html

The Economist: German Economy. www.economist.com/topics/german-economy

European Journalism Centre: Media Landscape—Germany. www.ejc.net/media_landscape/article/germany/

Facts About Germany: Political System. www.tatsachen-ueber-deutschland.de/en/political-system/main-content-04/the-federal-structure.html

German Culture: German History—All Facts and Events. www.germanculture.com.ua/library/history/bl_german_history.htm

The (German) Federal Environmental Agency. www.umweltbundesamt.de/index-e.htm

The (German) Federal Government. www.bundesregierung.de/Webs/Breg/EN/Homepage/_node.html

German Food Guide: German Cooking. www.germanfoodguide.com/cooking.htm

German Football Team. http://germanfootballteam.com/

Journey to Germany: The German Education System. www.journey-to-germany.com/education.html

MyGermanCity.com: The German Alps. www.mygermancity.com/german-alps

Newseum: The Berlin Wall. www.newseum.org/berlinwall/

Nazi Photos. http://nobeliefs.com/nazis.htm

NPR: Health Care for All—Germany. www.npr.org/series/91971170/germany-health-care-for-all

A Short Guide to the German Political System. www.rogerdarlington.me.uk/Germanpoliticalsystem.html

INDEX

Adorno, Theodor, 102
agriculture, 15, 24, 47, 49
airline, 49
Alps, 11—12, 15—17, 24v25, 52, 63, 72, 112, 115, 122
anti-Semitism, 85
architecture, 21—23, 72, 86, 106—107
Aryan, 35
autobahn, 48

Baltic Sea, 13, 33, 48, 66, 108, 112
bank, 22, 31, 34, 53, 60, 84
Bavaria, 10—11, 15—16, 19—20, 25—26, 46, 52, 60, 62, 65—67, 83, 91, 97, 109, 112—113, 116, 119, 122, 125—126, 129, 131
beer, 20, 115, 119, 125—126, 128—129
Berlin Wall, 19, 37—38
Bible, 84, 88, 100
Black Forest, 15, 64, 112, 115, 118
BMW, 21, 46, 49—50, 105, 107
bomb, 19, 23, 106
Bosch, 21
bread, 126—127
Brecht, Bertolt, 100—101
Bundestag, 41—44, 76

capitalism, 54, 101—102
canal, 13, 23, 48
car, 21, 49—51, 58—59, 87, 107, 113—114,
carnival, 117—118, 123
castle, 17, 25, 67, 69
cathedral, 80, 83, 106
children, 65, 68, 71, 73—74, 76—79, 91, 101, 109, 120, 127
cities, 20, 25, 47—48, 58, 65—66, 76, 95, 101, 110, 112
    Berlin, 19—21, 23, 25, 31—32, 34—40, 42—44, 47, 53, 62, 65—67, 74, 76, 78, 84—85, 88, 95, 98, 101, 103—104, 106—107, 115, 126

Dresden, 14, 19, 23, 56, 96
    Hannover, 19, 25, 47, 53, 121
    Munich, 16, 19—21, 23, 31, 46, 53, 66, 81, 95, 105, 107, 110, 112, 118—119, 123, 127
Cold War, 36—37, 45, 68
Cologne Carnival, 118, 123
communist, 19, 23, 36—37, 44, 82, 103
concentration camp, 35, 67
constitution, 19, 34, 38, 41, 44—45, 81
costume, 64, 66, 116—118, 120—121, 123
cuisine, 125—126, 128—129
currency, 36, 42, 48, 53

Danube, 15, 28, 48, 59, 112, 126
Daimler, 21, 50—51
debt, 47, 53, 55
democracy, 41, 44, 82
dirndl, 66

East Germany, 18—19, 38, 44—45, 47, 49, 54, 82, 85, 100, 106, 110, 113
economy, 18, 20, 23, 34, 37, 42, 45—48, 52—55, 60—61, 67, 78, 101, 115
education, 23, 43, 68—69, 74, 76—79, 83, 85, 96, 114
energy, 20, 25, 49, 57, 58, 61
Engels, Friedrich, 103
environment, 18, 43—44, 56—61, 63, 78
Ernst, Max, 105
European Union, 39, 51—53, 55, 59, 87, 129
euro, 53
eurozone, 47, 53
exports, 49, 52—53, 60—61

family, 34, 37, 50—51, 59, 66—67, 72—75, 91, 97, 114, 120
fancy dress, 117

farm, 16, 33, 52, 61, 127
fascist, 35, 101
festival, 66, 83, 85, 96—98, 100, 116—121, 123
food, 36, 47, 75, 112, 115, 119, 124—126, 128, 129,
football, 61, 71, 110—111, 115
forest, 14—16, 21, 24, 49, 51—52, 58, 62, 64, 78, 79, 112, 115, 118
Frankfurt, 6, 12, 15, 22, 47, 53, 65, 66, 84, 126

gingerbread, 120—121
government, 18—20, 22, 25, 34, 37, 38, 40—43, 45, 48, 52, 54, 57—60, 63, 67, 76, 82, 85, 95—96, 99, 104—105, 110, 129
greetings, 91, 93
Gutenberg, Johannes, 88, 100

handball, 110, 115
health, 43, 59, 68, 78—79, 104, 112
Hesse, Herman, 102
hiking, 112
Hitler, Adolf, 7, 34—35, 63, 67, 82, 85, 99, 101
holiday, 8, 109, 120
horses, 52, 112, 119, 121

IBM, 21
imports, 49, 51
industry, 14—18, 20—21, 24, 31, 44—45, 47—51, 57—59, 65, 68, 78, 99, 102—103, 109, 128—129

jobs, 7, 35, 44, 51, 55, 65, 68

Kafka, Franz, 102
kaiser, 32, 33, 90
Kandinsky, Wassily, 105
Kant, Immanuel, 102—103

law, 18, 25, 41—45, 55, 57—58, 68, 74—76, 81, 85, 103, 129

INDEX

Lent, 117—118
loden, 66
Luther, Martin, 30, 84—85, 100, 105, 120

Mann, Thomas, 102
marriage, 45, 64, 73—76, 82, 119
Marx, Karl, 102—104
Marxist, 101, 103
mask, 117—118
Mass, 83, 121
meat, 120, 124—127, 130
Mercedes-Benz, 49—51
Merkel, Angela, 39, 52—53, 61
mountain, 10—14, 16, 24—25, 62, 110, 112, 122—123
museum, 20, 95, 97, 104—105, 107

national park, 15, 25, 56, 62—63
Nazi, 23, 34—35, 55, 63, 66—67, 69, 85, 92, 99, 101—102, 105, 123
Nibelungenlied, 100
Nietzsche, Friedrich, 100, 104
Nobel Prize, 78, 102
North Sea, 13, 17, 48, 52, 61, 68, 88, 126
nuclear, 44, 61, 100

Oberammergau Passion Play, 122, 123
Oktoberfest, 119, 123
Olympic, 21, 110, 113, 115

painting, 105—106, 122
parliament, 34, 39, 41—44, 76, 89, 101
Poland, 12, 33, 35, 38
Polish, 34, 36, 62, 68
political parties, 43
    Alliance '90 / the Greens, 42—44, 61
    Christian Democratic Union, 39, 42—43, 85
    Christian Social Union, 42—43
    Free Democratic Party, 42—43

Left, the, 39, 42—43
    Piratenpartei, 43
    Social Democratic Party of Germany, 34, 39, 42—43
politics, 5, 8, 18, 23, 28, 30—31, 39—41, 43—45, 61, 65, 68, 76, 84—85, 100, 102—105, 118
pollution, 18, 24—25, 44, 57—60
Porsche, 21, 49, 51
procession, 118, 120—121, 123

rail, 20, 36, 54
recycling, 57—58, 60—61, 63
Reichstag, 40, 42
religion, 80—81, 85
    atheist, 85
    Christian, 28—30, 39, 42—43, 81—82, 84—85, 104, 117, 120—122
    Jewish, 34—35, 67—69, 81, 83—84, 104, 122
    Muslim, 66, 85
    Roman Catholic, 30, 65, 74—75, 80—85, 117, 120—121
    Protestant, 30, 65, 74, 81—85, 100, 120
restaurant, 63, 125—128
reunification, 23, 19, 38, 45, 49, 51—52, 54, 68, 82, 102, 111, 117
Rhine, 6, 12, 14—15, 17, 19, 23—25, 28, 30—31, 35, 44, 48—49, 52, 54, 59—60, 65, 72, 83, 97, 112, 120, 123, 128, 130
river, 12—15, 17, 23, 25, 28, 30—31, 36, 48, 56, 59—60, 88, 112

school, 74, 76—78, 82, 85, 101, 106, 110, 112, 114, 127
scientist, 11, 103
sea, 13, 15, 17, 25, 31, 48, 52, 61, 66, 68, 88, 108, 112, 115, 126
shopping, 70, 76
Siemens, 21, 54
skating, 113
socialist, 34, 37, 68, 82, 104

sports, 20—21, 50—51, 63, 71, 110, 112—115
stores, 72, 76, 81, 87, 127—128
supermarket, 76, 121

telecommunications, 23, 49, 54
television, 20, 92, 99, 107, 111, 113
theater, 66, 94—95, 97, 99—101, 122
tourist, 20, 63, 115, 119, 122
Tracht, 66
train, 48, 70
transport, 20—22, 36, 42, 48, 59
Turks, 66—67, 85, 128

unemployment, 45, 52—53, 55, 68
UNESCO, 114
United Nations, 23, 114
United States, 33, 35—36, 39, 45, 48, 50—51, 58, 79, 98—99, 101, 113
university, 74, 77—78, 91

vacation, 38, 73, 76, 112, 114—115
Volkswagen, 49, 51
votes, 30, 34, 39, 42—44, 110

waterway, 17, 48, 59—60, 113
West Germany, 5, 18v19, 22, 25, 36—39, 45, 47—48, 51, 68, 110
wine, 17, 120—121, 125—126, 128, 130
World Cup, 110—111
World War I, 32, 33, 50, 67, 100—101, 105
World War II, 19, 21, 23, 32, 35, 39, 47, 69, 82—84, 106
wurst, 124, 126—127

Yugoslav, 35, 68, 115, 128